Dear Jessica and our Friends from
The Barry Foundation,

Please Know how grateful
we are for the huge impact
you are making for the
children of Camp Heartland.

Your Kindness, generosity and
compassion will transform the
lives of hundreds of Kids
who suffer greatly.

With THANKS
and Best Wishes,

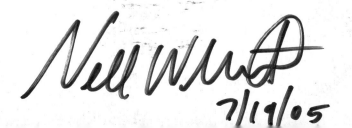

7/19/05

A Journey
of Hope

Inspiring Stories of
Courage and
Unconditional Love

By Neil Willenson
and the children of Camp Heartland,
a community of support for young people affected by HIV

Edited by Kurt Chandler

Photography by Katja Heinemann

Logan, age 10, with Patrick

Library of Congress Cataloging-in-Publication data is available.
ISBN 0-9767169-3-3
First Edition

Published in the United States by Camp Heartland Project, Inc.
Designed by Quantum Advertising & Design, Inc., Chicago, Illinois
Printed by Inland Book, LLC. Menomonee Falls, Wisconsin
Scans by Color Edge Art, NYC

Camp Heartland
www.campheartland.org
1845 N. Farwell #310 • Milwaukee, WI 53202
(414) 272-1118 • (800) 724-4673

"A Journey of Hope" is dedicated to:

Dawn Wolff and her children, Nile and Sean. Dawn will always be considered "the mother of Camp Heartland" and her children – now grown – remain my inspiration.

The two thousand children who have been a part of the Camp Heartland family. This book was difficult to write, as adequate words are hard to come by in describing your impact on me.

The dedicated staff, board and volunteers who have made it possible for our organization to grow and flourish. Although the spotlight may not often shine on you, you all should glow with the satisfaction of your many accomplishments.

My family for their tireless support. Many thanks to my wife, Adria, and newborn baby, Alanna Rose. Alanna's good health is a blessing that I will never take for granted.

Kurt Chandler and Katja Heinemann for their unwavering enthusiasm for this project. I am so very grateful for your many talents.

Many thanks to GE Healthcare and the Daniel M. Soref Charitable Trust for sponsoring our national Journey of Hope AIDS Awareness Tour. Thanks to you, all net proceeds will support Camp Heartland's programs.

This book can be considered a voice for our 60 campers who have died from AIDS complications. Your legacy is one that will live on through each chapter. I join the hundreds of camp counselors who fondly cherish their memories of you. Finally, I thank each reader for caring enough to turn the pages.

— NEIL WILLENSON

Table of Contents

Vincent and Jake, age 12

Neil with campers, summer 2002

My Unexpected Journey

By Neil Willenson

I sometimes wonder where I would be and what I would be doing had I not read a newspaper headline about 5 year-old Nile Sandeen. Nile was the first child I ever met with HIV. Befriending his mom, Dawn Wolff, and seeing her family's struggles firsthand, ultimately inspired the creation of the Camp Heartland charity.

> "I could have missed the pain, but I'd have had to miss the dance."
>
> —Garth Brooks

Without Camp Heartland I would have certainly missed the pain and devastation of losing dozens of children, eulogizing a child who I loved like a brother, and experiencing moments of absolute sorrow when I knew there was nothing I could do to ease a child's pain. Without a doubt, the saddest moments in my young life have involved children with AIDS.

By getting to know Nile, founding Camp Heartland and traveling the country with kids with AIDS, I have certainly set myself up for a huge amount of grief. Yet, there has never been a day when I regretted knowing and caring for these children.

Yes, I could have missed the pain, but I also would have missed the moments of great inspiration and joy, the moments when I knew Camp Heartland was making a tangible difference, the moments I gave love and received even more.

During my high school years when I imagined myself at age 34, I dreamed I would be a Hollywood producer, making movies – and making millions. I might not be making movies, but I'm proud to be a character in the lives of thousands of children. I may not be rich, but I have been exceedingly enriched by my unexpected career.

This is not the life I predicted for myself, but I thank God I met Dawn Wolff and her children. It has been an incredible privilege to be a small part of the personal journeys of these courageous kids.

"A Journey of Hope" provides you the opportunity to become familiar with the hopes, dreams and struggles experienced by children with AIDS and their families. I ask you to take your time with each page so you can truly absorb the substance of the children's stories, poems, and photographs. As it has for me, I guarantee "meeting" these kids will profoundly change and inspire you.

Hope in the Heartland

Awakening

By Neil Willenson

It is the fall of 1992. I'm on the phone with a soccer coach from my hometown of Mequon, Wisconsin. And I'm angry. Even though he is legally entitled to play, the coach refuses to allow my 7-year-old friend Nile Sandeen to join the youth soccer league. His older brother can play, but not Nile. Nile has AIDS.

"We're not equipped to deal with this child," the coach says. "What if there's an accident, a blood spill?"

"Youth soccer is not a contact sport," I tell the coach. "There aren't going to be any massive blood spills. And besides, you have no idea who is HIV positive and who is not. All you have to do is follow universal precautions…."

But it's no use. I realize the argument had been lost long before I made the phone call.

Nile was infected with HIV at birth through his mother, Dawn Wolff. When Nile was in kindergarten, his mother went public about their HIV status. She no longer wanted to live behind the veil of secrecy. But sadly, the family saw discrimination raise its ugly head again and again — discrimination based on fear and just plain ignorance.

"There must be other kids like Nile who want to make friends, have fun and talk about AIDS," I say to myself as I hang up the phone. "So where do they go? Where do they play?"

On New Year's Day, 1993, I set out to answer those questions. I decided to do something for Nile and other kids like him. My first day of that new year began with the birth of an idea: A summer camp for kids affected by HIV and AIDS.

The following summer, Nile finally got to play soccer — at the first day of the first Camp Heartland session. Among his teammates were his brother, Sean, who was not infected, and other children who had AIDS or were affected by the disease. They all were surviving AIDS in some way. They all needed a break from the stigma that often marks someone touched by the virus. And Camp Heartland was just the ticket. That day was a terrific victory for Nile and for me.

In its inaugural year, Camp Heartland welcomed 72 children to a seven-day summer camp at a leased campground near Milwaukee. Kids 7 to 17 from 20 states came to camp free of charge, funded by donations of money, goods and services. They fished, they hiked, they rode horses, they learned archery, they climbed trees — all of the joys of any other summer camp. Even more importantly, for the first time in their young lives they could speak openly about the disease.

One of the most memorable moments of my life came on the last night of camp in that first year. I was sitting under a tree with Nile, looking at the children from around the country, when I turned to him and said, "This is all because of you, Nile." From the smile on his face, I knew that he was pleased and proud that he had inspired the Camp Heartland organization.

My AIDS activism began, appropriately enough, at a summer camp. When I was in my early 20s, I worked as a senior counselor at a YMCA camp in the Pocono Mountains of Pennsylvania. A year earlier, I had read the book *My Own Story* by the late Ryan White, a teenager who was a leading international AIDS activist. I was stirred by Ryan's courage — how he had fought against the hateful prejudice that he'd encountered from the people in his hometown.

At the YMCA camp, I held "devotion time" for campers just before bed. I turned off the lights in the cabin, placed a candle on the floor in the middle of the room, and led discussions about all kinds of things. At most camps, devotion topics typically center on sports and camp events and joke telling. But I saw devotion time as a chance to teach kids about other cultures and social issues, and about being compassionate. It was challenging to strike a balance between kids who were informed and kids who were not.

Very often I read passages out loud from Ryan White's book. The campers were touched by Ryan's story. Many were moved to tears. In the dark, I could hear sniffling from the bunk beds. After my reading, I was bombarded with questions about HIV and AIDS. Their reaction was overwhelming. Clearly, this topic had struck a nerve with these children. I quickly realized that many of these kids had never talked about issues such as AIDS.

I always ended this devotion with a message: "If someone in your hometown has HIV or AIDS, you don't have to step back in fear. You can step forward and be their friend." All the children joined me in placing our hands together as we made a pledge to be kind to anyone we met with the disease.

Mequon-Thiensville Edition

OZAUKEE COUNTY

NEWS GRAPHIC

MONDAY, SEPTEMBER 9, 1991   VOL. 108 NO. 67   1 SECTION/28 PAGES   50 CENTS

AIDS hysteria
Oriole Lane parents fear for children's safety
By Steven Beuter

Ozaukee County News Graphic, 1991

Little did I know that less than a month later I would have the opportunity to practice what I preached. Late in the summer of '91, I returned from summer camp and was at my parents' home one day, walking through the house, when I tripped over a stack of newspapers. I looked down at my clumsy feet and noticed a headline from the local paper: "AIDS hysteria: Oriole Lane parents fear for children's safety."

It sounded as if a monster was on the loose. I sat down and read the article. It was a story about Nile.

I was outraged. How could my seemingly well-educated neighbors be so misinformed and hurtful?

The article really hit home. I had spent so many hours that summer reading to dozens of children about this disease. I recalled the pledge I made with the campers each week. With that in mind, I called up the family just to let them know I wasn't afraid of them, and that there was somebody in the community who did care about them. Almost immediately, I became friends with Nile, his brother Sean, and their mother Dawn.

After getting to know both brothers, it was clear to me that their suffering was not so much from the disease itself but from the stigma, paranoia and cruelty that too often surrounds HIV/AIDS.

This got me thinking: If Nile was badly treated for having HIV, there must be other children like him who were singled out, too. Who do these children turn to for support? Where do they go to get away from the cruelty and prejudice? And even though Sean was not living with HIV, he was certainly affected by the disease. His dad had died from AIDS, and without a medical miracle it appeared that Sean would be the sole survivor of his family. Clearly, children like Sean needed a place of openness and warmth where they could share their feelings as well.

As Founder and CEO of Camp Heartland, my vision has remained constant over the years: we want to provide kids who have been affected by HIV and AIDS with a place of total acceptance, a refuge from the judgment and isolation that they face every day, a retreat from the fear of the future, a safe haven where they can be themselves, where they can have fun and make friends. Not only does Camp Heartland have the typical summer camp activities but we also offer HIV discussion groups where kids can share their secrets.

My dream is a work-in-progress. Now in its 12th year, Camp Heartland has provided more than 5,000 camp experiences, welcoming children from all across the country to campgrounds in New Jersey, Illinois, Wisconsin, Missouri and California. Nile, now 19, was one of the regulars since the very beginning. The majority of our campers also live in poverty. But, through the generosity of thousands of donors, all of our programs and services are provided free of charge.

Within a few years of creating Camp Heartland it became quite clear that we needed a year-round home. I was pleased with the impact that we were making for hundreds of kids each summer, but the issues the kids faced needed to be addressed all year-long. Our vision grew from a week-long program into one of a year-round charitable organization that would make a profound life-long impact for children, teenagers and young adults affected by HIV/AIDS. But where would we find our year-round home?

In 1997, with the help of some tremendously generous

people including our spokesperson, baseball Hall-of-Famer Paul Molitor, we realized our ultimate goal — a permanent camp. An 88-acre camp was purchased. In the summer of 1998, the inaugural session was held at the Camp Heartland Center in Willow River, Minnesota.

Willow River is about 100 miles north of the Twin Cities on the road to Duluth. The town has a good hardware store, a barber shop, a school, a church, a bank, two or three bars, and a community fire hall. Not much else.

But the small community has warmly welcomed Camp Heartland. Despite some initial fears, the town eventually grew to understand — and accept — children with HIV/AIDS. Unlike many larger communities, where HIV paranoia still runs rampant, the residents of Willow River, through their compassion and common sense, have become Camp Heartland's greatest allies.

Since opening in 1998, the center has become a place that children affected by HIV and AIDS can come back to year after year, a place they can count on year-round for uncondi-tional love and acceptance. The Camp Heartland Center is the first of its kind anywhere in the world.

In addition to our camping programs, Camp Heartland goes on the road throughout the year with our

Nile, 1996; Nile and Chris, 1993

ongoing AIDS awareness tour, called "The Journey of Hope." I, along with other staff members, travel with children affected by HIV/AIDS to middle schools, high schools, colleges, churches and civic groups around the country, delivering a message of HIV prevention, acceptance, compassion, testing and hope. As over 100 of our campers have been trained as "HIV ambassadors," our message has reached tens of thousands so far.

Year to year, at each camp session and on each Journey of Hope tour, new stories unfold — stories of discrimination, of loneliness, of unjustifiable pain and suffering, of tragedy beyond belief. The life of a child with AIDS can be very lonely, sad and painful. But something else springs forth. Beyond the stories of suffering and tragedy spring stories of love, hope, courage, resilience and strength. There are even hopeful moments in the lives of the children who have died.

I have celebrated the birthdays of campers, and I have buried children. I have attended bar mitzvahs of kids with AIDS, and I have delivered their eulogies. I have laughed... and cried. Working with more than 2,000 children with HIV/AIDS has been marked by many contra-dictions. Some days my grief is so tangible it feels as if I have weights strapped to my body. But most days are filled with joy and inspiration. The very happiest are when I witness a life milestone for a child or a teenager with the disease.

Children who were once sad have found a renewed sense of hope and purpose. Children who were expected to live until their 10th birthdays are now finishing adolescence. Children who once had no friends are now getting married and having families of their own. Former campers have lived long enough to become camp counselors themselves.

In the 12-year history of Camp Heartland, I have seen these amazing stories unfold before my very eyes. *It is time for these stories to be told.* Turn the page and I will introduce you to two of these stories. You will meet Ryan and Jonathan, two of the 2,000 — two boys with AIDS who I met in our very first year. Although they are just two of the many children who have attended Camp Heartland, their stories illustrate the courage, struggles and hope of all of our campers.

Ryan and Jonathan grew to become best of friends and Camp Heartland regulars. But as you will see throughout this book, the virus affects each person in many different ways. And in the case of Ryan and Jonathan, AIDS delivered vastly different outcomes.

Ryan's Light

By Neil Willenson

It was Camp Heartland's first summer, and I was tense. "Would the kids get along with each other?" I asked myself. "Would they be in any danger? What if someone gets ill?"

No more than 10 minutes after the campers arrived, I got an urgent call on my walkie-talkie: "There's a kid in the infirmary already." I hurried over to "Club Meds," as we came to call it, and lying on a cot was this 10-year-old boy with big blood-shot eyes. It was clear that he was very sick.

"Hi, I'm Noodle," I said to him, using my camp nickname. "Welcome to Camp Heartland."

"I'm Ryan," said the boy, managing a smile. "I want to take a nap for a little while." And he drifted off to sleep....

Ryan was born on August 10, 1982, the first and only child of Mike and Debbie Chedester. The Chedesters lived in Whiteville, Louisiana, a community of about 200 people. Like many parents, Mike and Debbie didn't care if their child was a boy or a girl. They just wanted a healthy child.

Unfortunately, things didn't turn out that way.

After a difficult delivery, the doctor had dreadful news for Debbie and Mike. "Your child has severe internal bleeding. We don't know what it is or how to stop it. His chances of survival are very slim." Preparing for the worst, the Chedesters called their priest and asked him to baptize the baby. And they asked him to perform the Last Rites.

But this miracle baby wanted to live. Somehow he survived Day One, and then Day Two, and Day Three and Day Four. The bleeding was controlled, and after six weeks, Ryan was released from the hospital.

Around the sixth month of his life, Ryan's parents noticed that he was bruising very easily. He had trouble learning to sit up, and his joints began swelling. The doctors diagnosed Ryan with hemophilia, a genetic blood-clotting disorder that can be exceptionally painful. Like all hemophiliacs, Ryan would be prone to severe swelling and bleeding around the joints.

As he grew into a toddler, at the insistence of his physician, Ryan's parents began giving him a blood product, Factor VIII — made partly from donated blood plasma. In some ways it was a life-saving product. His mother could give him Factor VIII through an infusion, and his blood would clot at a normal level if he were injured.

But there was a problem with the medication, an awful problem. Before 1982, neither the drug manufacturers nor the government knew that some of the blood used to make Factor VIII had been contaminated with HIV. And when they finally did find out, they delayed in announcing the danger until 1985. Unbeknown to hemophiliac patients, some of their treatments were tainted with HIV.

Ryan was told by his mother that he had HIV when he was 9. It was an enormously difficult thing for Debbie to do — to sit down and essentially deliver a death sentence to her child. But at that time, there was very little hope for people with AIDS.

Ryan's family decided to kept the news a secret. They were worried about a potentially negative reaction by his teachers and classmates and neighbors. They remembered another Ryan — Ryan White, the boy from Kokomo, Indiana, who had been shunned by his friends and banned from public school. So they kept the news to themselves. Only Ryan's immediate family and grandparents knew he was HIV positive.

In 1993, as summer approached, Ryan signed up for Camp Heartland. He was frightfully ill at the time with pneumocystis carinii pneumonia, a common illness for people with AIDS and a frequent cause of death. Breathing was nearly impossible for Ryan.

Again, Ryan prevailed. He survived the pneumonia. But his immune system suffered terribly. His T4-cells — a indicator of the state of the immune system — fell to a dangerously low level. For most people, a normal T4-cell count is over 1,000. Ryan had less than 10.

Yet he had made up his mind. "I want to go to camp," he told his parents. "I want to have some fun for awhile...."

Ryan awoke from his nap after two or three hours. He was restless.

"I need to get out of bed and do something," he said. "That's why I came here, to have fun."

For the rest of that day, Ryan played football, mastered the climbing wall, and went canoeing. His shaggy brown hair flopped over his forehead as he ran from one activity to the next, and his grin turned wider and wider as the day went on.

After dinner, he was back in bed, worn out but happy. He had made dozens of new friends, people just like him, people with HIV and AIDS who simply wanted to have fun.

On the third night of camp, we held a small candlelight ceremony before the kids went to bed. In a circle, we lit a single candle and passed it around. Each child had a chance to speak. Ryan was shy. But when the candle was passed to him, he looked at his fellow campers, nodded his head and said, "You know, this is the best week of my life."

At that moment, I knew that Camp Heartland would be a success....

Even though he was very ill, Ryan had a great week, seven days of pure, worry-free fun. Hampered by an overwhelming fatigue, he missed many camp activities. But it didn't really matter. He was liberated. Coming to Camp Heartland and

Ryan, age 12

meeting a group of young people who were not afraid to play football with him, to share meals with him, to hug him — it was just what he needed.

Ryan went home from camp empowered. Sure, he was from a great family and went to a good school. But the secret that he was forced to live with made him a prisoner in his own hometown. "I'm tired of living a lie," he told his mother when he got home. "I want to tell my neighbors and my friends. If they don't like me for who I am, then they weren't really my friends to begin with. I want to tell the whole world I have AIDS."

And he did just that. Ryan began speaking out at school and in the local media, sharing this painful secret about his illness. Soon, all of Whiteville knew that Ryan had AIDS. As the news began to spread, he appeared with me on the "CBS Morning Show," and millions knew.

The people of Whiteville did not step back in fear. They were not angry, they were not suspicious. Instead, they took the time to learn about HIV. With words and actions, they assured him, "We're not afraid of you, Ryan. You will always be our friend." That small town stepped up and made a lifelong commitment to help and support Ryan Chedester, because he was one of their own.

Ryan, age 10, with Neil

Basking in the support of his family and community, Ryan was a carefree boy. He loved fishing. He loved riding his four-wheeler. He loved sports, video games, Beavis and Butthead. He would float around in a swimming pool for hours without interruption. He drank so much Dr Pepper I wanted to buy stock in the company. Ryan was a kid living with AIDS. But first and foremost, he was a kid.

In August of 1995, Ryan was struck down with cryptosporidium, a water-borne parasite that he contracted by drinking tap water in his town. Ryan and his mother received the news of his illness while at a Camp Heartland session in California. Ryan's prognosis was grim. He was as ill as anyone I've ever seen. This was AIDS, this was hemophilia, this was cryptosporidium — all combined. No one deserved to go through that.

For six months, off and on, Ryan stayed at Tulane University Hospital in downtown New Orleans. Whenever I would visit, I tried to take his mind off his pain and despair. Sometimes his mom and I would sneak him out of the hospital and we would go shopping or to a movie or just drive around town, his mother behind the wheel and Ryan wedged between us in the front seat. Even if it was just an hour, it was good for him to get out.

On one visit, Ryan was especially fidgety. "I've got an idea," he told me as he gazed out the window of his room. "How 'bout if we go up to the roof and drop some water balloons?"

His puppy-dog eyes twinkled with excitement. How could I deny him? We devised a plan: We would sneak up to the top of the parking garage and shower the pedestrians below with a friendly little downpour.

Ryan could barely walk, so we squeezed him into a red hospital wagon, wrapped him in a blanket, and stuffed dozens of bulging water balloons under the blanket. Then, holding back the giggles and acting as nonchalant as we could, we glided past the security guard, whistling — just like in the movies. Then we bolted for the elevator. Up we went with our wagon of water balloons to the top of the parking garage. And, in broad daylight, balloon after balloon rained down on the streets of New Orleans.

Ryan absolutely loved it. It was a great moment, and one of last times I saw him. It is a day I will hold onto forever....

I saw a play a while ago called "The Yellow Boat," written by David Saar about his son, a boy with hemophilia and AIDS. During the play, the boy tells a Scandinavian folk tale about three colored boats on the ocean. According to the legend, the red boat carried faith, the blue boat carried hope, and the yellow boat carried love. At the end of the day, the red boat sailed back to the harbor, along with the blue boat. But the yellow boat sailed up to the sun.

I can imagine Ryan Chedester telling his parents, "Daddy, you be the red boat, and Mama, you be the blue boat. But I will be the yellow boat."

Ryan's yellow boat has sailed to the sun, his yellow boat has sailed to the heavens, his yellow boat has sailed to God. And Ryan's light will shine on us for many years to come.

An Epilogue: Blue Pacific Memories

In 1998, two years after Ryan's death, his mother Debbie returned for a week-long session at Camp Heartland in Malibu, where she volunteered as a nurse. She was filled with mixed emotions, coming back to the place where Ryan spent so many happy days – and the place where he was diagnosed with cryptosporidium.

Dwayne, Debbie's significant other, knew she would be silently grieving. So he accompanied her to Camp Heartland and worked as the camp's transportation coordinator.

On a beautiful California evening, as the sun sank gloriously into the Pacific, Dwayne asked Debbie to be his bride. She accepted, and the engagement was announced to the entire camp at dinner. Everyone cheered.

"I want her sad memories to be offset with happy memories," Dwayne smiled.

Ryan's Poem

I believe in angels
Don't you see
They are all around us
Watching after you
And taking care of me

They are helping you travel
Very very far
The twinkle of your eyes
Will be seen in the stars

Look at the moon
There is your smile
Kids all over the world
Will see it for miles and miles

I believe in angels
Don't you see
They are God's helpers
Taking the pain away
From you and me

I love you Ryan
— STEPHANIE, AGE 10

Jonathan

DEFYING THE EXPERTS

By Neil Willenson

When Jonathan Swain was born in March of 1983, HIV was still considered "the gay disease." In the minds of the medical experts, HIV only infected people on the East and West Coasts. People from middle America like Denver, where Jonathan and his family lived, were considered safe.

Jonathan was born 6 and ½ weeks prematurely and given blood transfusions. At the time, the nation's blood supply was not tested for HIV, and Jonathan was infected with the virus.

In the first two years of his life, Jonathan faced bouts of pneumonia, bacterial infections, pinkeye, along with countless, agonizing tests, including biopsies of the liver, lungs and lymph nodes. He was tested for numerous diseases, but never for HIV.

On a dark day in 1985, Jonathan's doctors finally determined he was living with AIDS. They told his mother, Shiela, that her young son would never see his sixth birthday.

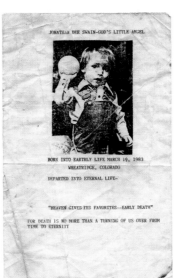

Obituary, 1985

So Shiela put together a funeral announcement for Jonathan and prepared for his imminent death.

For the first few years, Shiela kept Jon's illness a secret from all but her closest loved ones. In 1986, there wasn't much compassion for those with AIDS. Even as he suffered the daily pain of the disease and the uncomfortable side effects of the medicines, Jon still wanted to be a normal little boy. He made some friends and tried to have fun.

One day while playing in the yard, he told all the other little boys, "I have AIDS!" They thought it was "pretty cool" and made sure they told their mommies all about it.

In short order, Jonathan and Shiela were surrounded by controversy. So Shiela shared the family secret and worked to educate the community.

Jonathan was the first child with AIDS in the country to go to public school without a court order, thanks to Shiela's steadfast efforts at AIDS awareness. A book was published, *My Name is Jonathan and I Have AIDS,* and Jon visited Japan with his family to promote HIV education and prevention. He became something of a celebrity, the "Ryan White of Japan," an inspiration to thousands of children.

Yet some people were mean — even to a little boy. His neighbors told Jonathan not to swim in the swimming pool where he and Shiela lived. Some so-called "religious" people in their community kicked the Swains out of two churches that they had attended. They wouldn't let Jon play with their children. Not only did he suffer from AIDS, but he suffered the slings and arrows of ignorance and cruelty.

Nevertheless, Shiela and her son had a good reason to celebrate: Jonathan did in fact live to see his sixth birthday. And somehow, he continued to grow and grow, just another kid with the same kind of hopes and dreams....

When he was 10, Jonathan came to Camp Heartland with his brother, Josh. For the first time ever, Jonathan felt totally free. He was accepted. He was with other children, like Ryan

Chedester, who understood what he was going through. Like so many others, he had the time of his life.

Months later, Jonathan joined me on our Journey of Hope programs, touring the country and encouraging young people to stay HIV free. After one particular speech, as I drove him to the airport, I asked him what his dream was. I expected him to say something about being a professional football player. But instead, without a pause, he said: "My dream in life is to live to be 20."

It appeared that Jonathan's dream would be just that — an unachievable dream. Medicines were very limited in the early 1990s. As a result, Jon lost five of his best friends to AIDS, including his first girlfriend, Sara. Imagine watching your friends die of the same disease that you have inside your own body.

But ground-breaking medicines were soon developed. Protease inhibitors gave Jon and thousands of other people with AIDS renewed health and hope. Jonathan got healthier. He continued fighting ignorance, and he continued coming to camp.

Yet, on occasion he still suffered the ill effects of ignorance. During his senior year in high school, he took a dip in a friend's

ABOVE: Jonathan at camp, 1994
BELOW RIGHT: Jonathan and family, 2004

Jacuzzi and swimming pool. Upon finding out that Jon had HIV, the father of Jon's friend had both pools completely drained and cleaned. HIV cannot be transmitted in a pool; the behavior was completely irrational. Yet these kinds of incidents follow nearly every young person with AIDS.

Despite the misunderstandings, Jon tried to live the life of a "normal" teenager — except for the 20 pills he took each day, except for the monthly doctor visits, except for the painful medical procedures, except for the discrimination, except for the loss of his best friends to AIDS, except for the fact that he had to struggle every day to have some sense of comfort and acceptance.

And so Jon moved forward with his life one day at a time.

As he was nearing the completion of his senior year at Homestead High School in Mequon, Wisconsin, Jon's family and friends anticipated his upcoming graduation ceremony. His

brother, Troy, and sister-in-law, Dana, flew in from San Francisco. They were joined by Jon's grandparents from Iowa. Taking the last of the few remaining coveted tickets were some of my friends and co-workers who had met Jon through Camp Heartland.

As I watched Jon walk across the stage to receive his diploma, I nearly burst with pride. I cannot think of a young person who had overcome as many obstacles.

A year later, one of my own dreams came true in December of 2002, when Jon served as a groomsmen at my wedding to Adria. At the reception, he offered a toast, speaking candidly about the impact that I made on his life. I was deeply moved, and flattered by his gratitude. But I also know that Jon is the strongest person I have ever met.

Two weeks before Jonathan's twentieth birthday, I made a large framed collage of many of his photos, newspapers articles, and even his funeral announcement written by his mother. After seeing so many children succumb to AIDS, I was thrilled that Jon would meet his goal of "living to be 20." The collage now hangs in Jon's home in Utah, a testament to all of the issues that he has faced head on. He is the very definition of a survivor.

Now 22, Jon takes his medicines, doesn't drink or smoke, studies, works hard, lifts weights daily and owns his own home. More impressively, Jon is married to a wonderful woman, Amber, and they have a new, healthy baby together, Jett Davis Swain. Although Jon was always optimistic, I don't believe he ever foresaw the day when he would be 22 years old, married and have his own baby son. There truly is hope!

And, oh yes, he has a new goal in life: To live to be 80.

Somehow, I know he'll make it.

A Lesson in Survival

By Neil Willenson

When I founded Camp Heartland and befriended hundreds of children living with AIDS, I knew I was setting myself up for an unimaginable amount of grief. After my mother became educated about HIV and realized I wasn't going to contract it from the children, she seemed to worry far more about my emotional health.

"Neil," she said, "you're setting yourself up for such sadness."

She was right. On a daily basis, I wondered and worried about the loss of the children I cared about so deeply. Yet, I never held anything back from the kids. I knew there would be painful times ahead but I viewed every moment with the children as valuable for them — and me.

Our entire volunteer staff experienced the sobering reality of AIDS when a young boy named Brandon died the day before our inaugural camp session in 1993. We realized very quickly that we didn't have the luxury of time with these kids. If we were going to make an impact on their lives, we needed to do it immediately.

Since the loss of Brandon, we have grieved for 60 other Camp Heartland children. As I have traveled the country speaking about pediatric AIDS, I've shared stories of the campers who have died. Each of them had a unique personality with a story that deserves to be shared. Each of them died decades before their time.

In the early years of the camp I often wished we could freeze the happy moments in time — moments like the spontaneous water fights, where 150 kids and volunteers soaked each other with wild abandon. For many of the kids whose minutes and hours were dictated by complicated medication regimens, this was one time that was completely carefree.

I wish we could give years of our own lives to the kids, in order to extend their lives. If I was going to live to be 80, I could give up 10 of my years to a child with AIDS. Seventy years is still a nice life compared to a child with a fatal disease.

Nile and Neil, summer 2002

When you work with children who are ill, it is frustrating knowing that you cannot ease the physical ravages caused by their disease. It's difficult to resign yourself to the fact that there still is no cure for the virus that infects their little bodies.

But at Camp Heartland, instead of shrugging our shoulders, we have focused on how we can make a difference — the emotional well being of these kids. We believe that by providing them with a renewed sense of hope and purpose, and increasing their self-esteem, we help them become physically stronger as well.

I believe this without a doubt. I have witnessed the growth of dozens of our campers from little children to grown adults. Through medical progress and their own determination, they have matured and become healthier. A community of supportive, loving people can make a profound impact. I grieve for those children who have died, but I look forward to celebrating many milestones with the children, teenagers and young adults who are now surviving AIDS.

Reflections

Noodle

When I'm at camp, my nickname is "Noodle," a term of endearment taken long ago from a cartoon character.

One summer, a 9-year-old boy named Bruce confided in me during rest time. Bruce was HIV free, but his father was living with AIDS.

"Noodle?" he whispered, his wide, dark eyes looking up at me. "If my daddy dies and my mom likes you, will you take his place? Will you be my daddy?"

"Bruce, I would be lucky to have a son like you," I said, without hesitation. "Anybody would. Your dad is doing okay, though. And I think he will be here for a long time."

Minutes later, he was outside laughing, spraying his fellow campers (and me) with a garden hose in the summer sun.

For the remainder of his camp trip, this boy was able to focus on having fun, but without hiding from the very real — and very scary — world of AIDS. Like other kids, he obviously had worries about himself and his family. And he was able to talk openly his worries.

Camp Heartland never shields kids from the realities of AIDS. To the contrary, we educate campers about the risks of HIV and about ways to live and even thrive with the virus. For Bruce, just talking about the virus did him a world of good.

— NEIL

Counting

I thought that I went through a lot
But when I open up my eyes and listen
There's a lot to be taught.

I realize that I'm lucky
When I thought that I was actually not.
I used to say everyone keeps leaving me,
But now I thank God for the ones he let stay.

I look around and see kids without parents
Then think: what would I do without mine?
Would I be able to pull through like my friends did?
I would probably break down and cry.

Looking around makes me wise,
Teaching me the real meaning
Of Counting my Blessings.

I could go and say
How I thank God for me not having HIV/AIDS
But even though I'm not, I'm affected in almost the same way.

So this is my thought:
I am willing to be taught.
I thought my life was challenging
But my friends at camp taught me a lot.
— DJ, AGE 16

Blessings

Vincent and Jake, age 12

You Never Know

When I found out she had it
I was young at the time.
If Jerome recalled the moment
He was about eight or nine.

I knew what it was but I had no clue
That Mama broke it down to me when the skies
  were blue.
Mickey D's afternoon in '95 was the year
I felt like crying, breaking down into tears.

In shocked disbelief, like — how could this be?
Was it the drugs or was it just Mom's stupidity?
Foster home for two years, so campers I know
  how you feel
Seein' ya moms everyday taking needles and poppin' pills.

It hurt like hell and it won't go away
Not moving to the west state, you just can't escape.
Somebody trade places with me, somebody pinch me and wake me up
Even if I stay up and think about times, still gon' be ruff.

I hate that it came about, I wish there was a real cure
What happened over there in Africa, how come blood ain't pure?
You know I feel them teardrops running down our cheeks
  when I speak
Now you know that this young man ain't weak.

Don't take me for granted, went from a boy to a man
I love the hell out of the person that invented Camp Heartland.

— JEROME, AGE 16

Most of the Time

I am 11 years old and I attend middle school in Virginia. I am on the A/B honor role. I love Greek Mythology, I take tae kwon doe classes and I take gymnastics classes. I recently joined a nice church and I want to join their choir because I love to sing.

I have AIDS, and to tell you the truth, I hardly remember it most of the time.

My birth mother was HIV positive and that's how I got it. I did not know about it until Mom and Dad told me, when I was 6 years old. They had to tell me then because I had to start taking medicine every day.

At first I was very scared. I was afraid to go to sleep at night in case I would not wake up. When I first started taking the medicine it made me very sick to my stomach.

I have a great doctor, Dr. Morrell, she's from Georgetown Hospital — she's French, and talks funny, but she is very kind to me and has taken care of me since I was two years old.

I may have AIDS but I am determined to live my life without worrying about dying.

I mean, my life is a whole lot better than some people. I have a family that loves me and a doctor who always takes care of me.

I have the talent of dance and love the arts. It makes me aware of what I am capable of.

I have experienced prejudice. People are still so scared of AIDS even though the disease is now at least 20 years old.

— MATTHEW, AGE 11

RayRay

Age 13

Some say my mother was getting around and all that. Some say she was taking drugs. But my father's family says she never took drugs, she never drank alcohol, but she got raped by her uncle, and that's how she got it.

And then I was born, and my mother died when I was 3, and I remember seeing her before she died. I saw her in her hospital bed. I didn't see my daddy any more after that. The year after my mother died he split us up, he took my brother to the white side of the family and me to the black side, because I had HIV, and the white side, they want nobody with HIV.

He always said he'd come and get me — but he died when I was 5, and he never came.

I talked to him the day before he died, and he was like: "I'm coming to get you tomorrow." And I was like: "Okay, you know, I'm packing my bags up, I'm ready to leave." And then my auntie told me, she's like: "Listen, your daddy died." And I just sat there all day and I just cried.

Then I got into a foster home when I was like 10 or 11 — I'm still in my foster home with my foster mother. She takes her daughter's side most of the time, 'cause that's her blood daughter. She always rules her daughter over me, it seems like. When I see them together, most of the time I just go in my room and cry, 'cause I'm like, why me? I don't look like none of them, so I don't feel like I fit in. They're darker than me, they look nothing like me and I just feel disowned, and my family won't even talk to me.

My brother told me that my aunt said she hope I don't take nobody down like my momma did, like give 'em AIDS — but my momma didn't know that she had it. She said she hope I don't take nobody down like my momma, and my momma, she slept around and stuff. That's what she say. But I don't believe her. I believe my daddy's side of the family.

Friends

Written with a pen
Sealed with a kiss
If you are my friend
Please answer this

Are we friends or are
We not?
You told me once but
I forgot

So tell me now and
Tell me the truth
So I can say
I am here for you

Of all the friends
I've ever met
You're the one
I won't forget

So if I die before
You do
I'll go to heaven
And wait for you!

— RayRay

Fire fire every were fire fire in my heart fire dont let me start to get aids like my mom its kind of Sad in this heart because if my mom dies I'll be Sad I cry forever and because my dads in Jail and I dont know were I'm going Please fire go away so I dont feel Sad any way

—chanel

:: camp Heart land

My Life

*My life is soooo hectic it hurts deep
  inside
To wake up every mornin' and think
  my brother might die
I feel so sorry for him to lie with this
  awful disease
Then I look at him and all fear is
  swept away
He's undetectable for the eighth time
  in a row
I look at him again and then I know
God is with him everywhere he goes
  then a peace comes over me in
  my soul
Then I look up to heaven and thank
  God he's alive
Then I hear a voice in my heart
  saying I'll be with him at all times*

— Lauren, age 12

Roses are red, violets are blue—and your feet are cold in the morning

— DEAH, AGE 7

A Poem on Colors

The grass is green
And the leaves are green too.
I'm a beautiful brown girl
And my mom is too.
The rainbow is full of
different colors
— DARLESHA

Illness

Why do I have this illness?
Where did it come from?
How did I get it?
Is there a cure?
Why does it have to be a secret from
*   relatives and friends?*
How long does this illness last?
A lifetime.
Do I have to live my life in lies?

Why, why, why?
I wish there was no HIV/AIDS.
This illness is making my life
*   terrible.*
All these question are in my head
I can only express on paper
Not to anyone else.
— BRITANI, AGE 13

DRAWING
by Brenda

Avyannah

HIV AND MY FRIEND'S

Hiv and my friend's just don't get along. I don't know why but I'm going to cry. I have no friends. You know why? I have Hiv and people laugh at me and call me names. So why do people do that? I just want to know? think about others not just your self.

By: Stacey
Age 12

My mom and my dad, they did cocaine and heroin and stuff and it passed on through the blood stream and into my body and I got it when I was born. And then a little while after, my mom and my dad died from it. Well, my mom did, but not my dad. My dad died from drugs. When I was born, the doctors said I was gonna live till, like, two. Well, they were wrong. I am now 14. I lived till, like, this age, so I'm really happy that I lived and I didn't die.

Stacey

If people wanna disrespect me, that's their fault. Because they didn't really get to know me, they just know my disease.

DRAWING by
Stacey, age 12

Another Day

Here it is another day
When she is sick once again.
And once again I sit and pray
To see her live another day.
I sit and wonder why.
Why has this been put upon us?
What did we do to deserve this?
And will it ever go away?
At times I stand outside watching her at play
Waiting and hoping for another day.

— SARAH, AGE 16

Positive

I don't really remember a lot, but I remember going to take my blood test. This is before my mom died, I was like 7 or 8. And we were there and we found out, my brother found out that he was negative, and I found out that I was positive, and all I know is positive sounds like a good thing, so I was like all happy. I'm like yeah, I'm HIV....You know, so I was all happy about being positive.

— ANONYMOUS

Diamond, age 8, takes his HIV medications

Abacovir...Bactrim...Epivir... Videx...Motrin...Viracept.

And I take Tylenol, and that's it. No liquids! Oh, and I take sleeping pills.
I take 'em two at a time.

Twice a day, I take the same amount at night, too — sometime.

Sometime I don't. Want me to tell you my secret? I hate taking medicine. Because it's not fun. Taking it every day!

At home sometimes I miss it. Sometime... I get in trouble if I lie to (my mom) and tell her I take it, but if I just tell her that I had missed, she won't get me in trouble. She'll tell me: start back on it. I don't miss all the time, I miss like one, like I miss the morning and take the night, or I miss the night and take the morning. I don't know why, 'cause it just feels like I take 'em and take 'em, thousands of pills every day.

My mom takes pills, but it's not for the same reason, she takes her vitamins. She takes hers every day, she don't miss not a day, she's just gulp, gulp....

I haven't been taking these for a very long time. I have been taking these for a year, but I have other meds I've been taking. I have been taking 'em for at least... all my life. I have been changing changin', changin', changing, because other medicines don't work for me.

They make my viral load go low, real low, and my T-cells go high, real high.

And the doctor says that's good. Then they say mine is undetectable. That means they can't find the virus in me. That's it.

They were trying to get me one of them things (a gastro-tube) —
I said uh-uh.

They said they wanna put one in my stomach, I said uh-uh. I said: You is not touching my stomach! My momma said it too. 'Cause I'm gaining weight on my own.

My cousins are like 10 times bigger than me, and they ain't nothing but 4,5 years old. We took a picture in Myrtle Beach... I looked so skinny. I had a bathing suit on, I looked so skinny and taut, compared to them two. I was real skinny. And they all catching up with me, with my weight. I'm supposed to be the one that's in my hundreds. But my cousin, he drank my (booster) juices. That boy's getting big...

— PEACHES, AGE 13

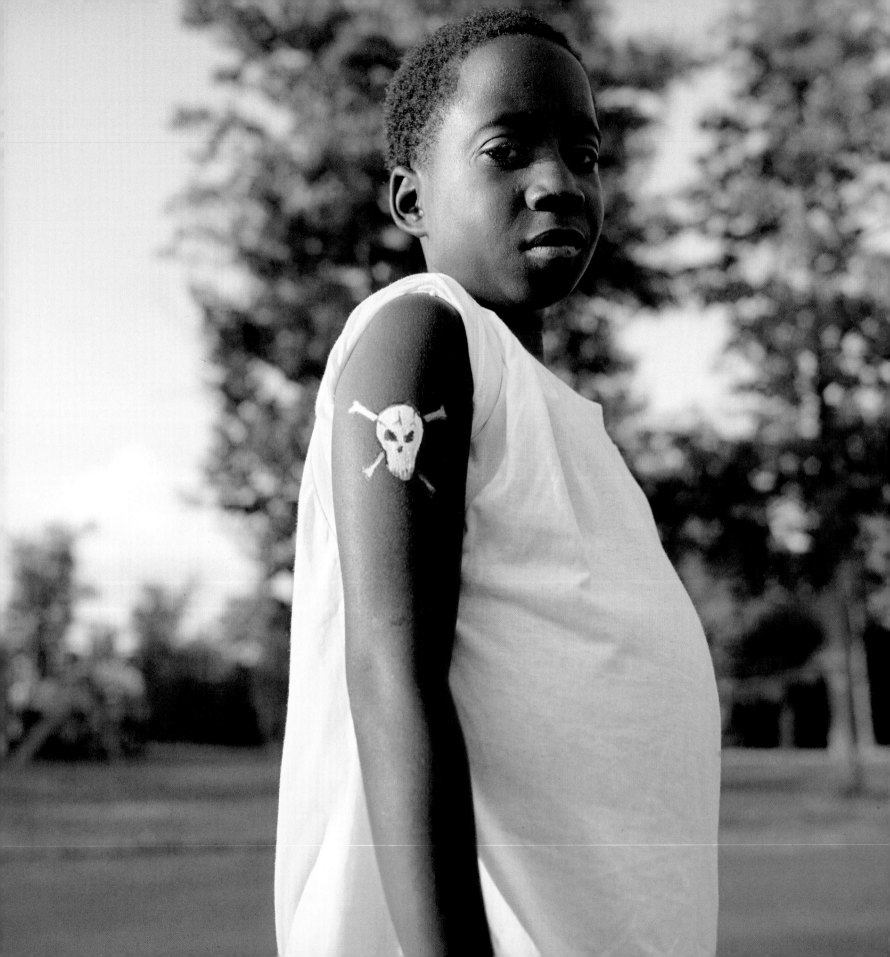

Why Me?

Why me,
Why did my mom have to have AIDS?
Why me,
Why did my mom have to die and leave me?
Why me,
Why do I have to be quiet & keep it to
* myself?*
Why me,
Why can't I tell my friends?
I don't know why
But I'm me
And you're you
And I'm strong and I'm normal
Just like you.

— ALISHA

Does It Matter?

Does it matter if we are black or white?
Does it matter if we're boy or girl?
Does it matter if the world knows that we have
* HIV/AIDS?*
It does not matter at all!
It does not matter at all!
Why do we care if it matters, we're all equal!

— BRITANI, AGE 13

Charisse's Story

I'm 11. My dad is infected. My mom is not.

When my dad gets sick there's nobody to take me anywhere. It's sad for me to watch him like that. But I'm not mad. It makes my dad special 'cause he has HIV…

Sometimes I help my dad take his meds. Sometimes he forgets…

Some people don't understand HIV, and people make fun of us. It really sucks. Some people think you can catch it just by looking at them…

— CHARISSE, AGE 11

DRAWING by
Darrel, age 14

Tabius, age 12

**DRAWING BY
STEPHON, AGE 13**

(Drawing text: "I hate HIV and AIDS")

Keeping Secrets

What really sucks in my school, like, a lot of kids make ignorant comments about it. And so it really hurts but you can't say anything back. You want to defend, but you can't really defend. It always sucks, like, some of my friends, not good friends, but some friends will make jokes about it and stuff like that, about people with the disease, so that sucks sometimes. 'cause they just don't understand, you know, so I can't really be mad at them, 'cause they just don't understand.

I mean, it sucks when you have to ask a question. Like, ask your doctor, can I do this with a girl or can I do that with a girl? You know. And then sometimes you get answers that you don't wanna hear.

I'm just gonna try to keep it secret as long as I can, at least throughout high school, that way I can get out there, and then probably want to try to get through college. And through my job. Until people start opening their minds or there's a cure or whatever. But I'm just gonna try to keep it a secret as long as I can. That way it doesn't affect my life and the way I wanna live. 'cause I'm trying not to make it affect my life.

— ANONYMOUS, AGE 16

Why?

Why did AIDS have to happen to me?
It affected my life, oh don't you see.
Why is the world unfair in a lot of ways,
Like why did my family have to get AIDS?
There are some questions I have been asking my entire life
Because there's no answer
It's like sitting on a plane
And going on and on in endless flight.
Why is AIDS upon this earth?
I really wish it had no birth.
But why did my sister have to get AIDS?
That "why" does bother me in a lot of ways.
I never thought it would happen to me —
WHY?

— TYREE, AGE 13

Erin, age 15

Every Part of My Life

I am 12 years old and am in sixth grade. My older brother and I live in California with our Gram and our Gramp, since our mother passed away in 1992, when she was barely 22 years old.

I can't remember too much about my mom, but I do remember going to the boardwalk with her and having lots of fun. It still makes me so sad on Mother's Day, or when I have to hear all my friends talk about all the things they do with their mothers. I never got to go to the movies, or camping, or anything like that with my mom. I didn't have her here to take me to school the first day I started. When I'm hurt or scared she's not here to sit and hold me or talk to. I never had the privilege of all this because of AIDS!

It's hard to talk about myself or my life without the subject of HIV and AIDS, since it has to do with every part of my life — from what I wear, what I eat and what I can or can't do, like sports and other activities. I feel like I am a "special" kid — and not in a good way. Being "special" in my life means always being different. I hate having to take 18 to 20 pills a day and having to have IV-IG treatments and needles stuck in me every three weeks. I can't even play sports anymore because it makes me too tired and runs my system down too much. It is sometimes very boring.

When my mom was 17, and seven months pregnant with me, she was told she had AIDS. For four years before she died, she tried her very best to help educate other young people so it might save their lives. Since that time my Gram has taught my brother and me how special our mom was and how proud we should always be of her. We have tried to take up where she left off to help educate young people about unprotected sex and drug users how important it is to NEVER use dirty needles. We also work to educate all people about this disease and help them to understand that we are no different than them.

I feel I have been very lucky in my life, even with having to deal with this disease, as I have met so many good people who really do care. But I know that there are other people, and especially other kids, who have not been so lucky. They are alone without the support and love that I have had all my life. We need to find them and help them too, and that is what I want to do with the rest of my life.

— AUGIE, AGE 12

My Name Is...

LaToya

Age 12

Sometimes when my birthday used to come, my auntie used to wake up and cry, because the doctor said I was gonna die at the age of 6. But then after I passed the age of 6, that's when we started celebrating my birthday.

My auntie told me I had it when I was 5 or 6. She explained to me what it is. But first she had to get herself educated, and then she explained to my family that it's in the house… I drink out of my auntie's cup, I hug everybody in my house.

My dad passed away when I was born. He didn't know he had it. He got it through unprotected sex and my momma passed it on to me when she was having me. The first time she knew was when I was sick and in the hospital, and they wanted to test me for HIV. She was like: No, she don't have that. And I tested positive, so she had to educate herself.

I used to take some nasty medicines, like Bactrum, and this other one… As a kid, every time I had to take Bactrum, I used to run from the room and hide in the closet, 'cause I didn't wanna take the Bactrum, 'cause it was so nasty! I take pills now. I used to take liquids, just started (taking pills) when I was 11.

Now I am 12. When I was younger, people used to call me names… I used to go home crying. But I didn't cry in school. Then when I got older they started seeing me like on TV and in the newspaper. They'd come up and ask me what is it, and I'd explain, and then they would understand, and then they wouldn't call me those things any more. I would tell them you can't get it from hugging, kissing, showing some love, or touching somebody — I just tell 'em it's in my blood. When I get a cut and you mix your cut with mine then you might get HIV, but I don't wanna do that, because I don't want to put this disease on anybody else.

I've been speaking a lot. I've been in newspapers since I was 2 years old. People ask: Am I afraid of dying? No! I don't wanna worry about that. All up in my business! Sometimes I just don't wanna answer them.

In Indiana, they call me the Northwest Indiana AIDS-child because I educate, and nobody else out there don't wanna say anything. They just don't wanna. They're probably afraid.

SHERIDAN: At school, when people go around talking about my mom, like they start cracking, then I don't have to take that, I just go off at 'em, start fighting them. That's why I'm always out of school. 'Cause I always fight so much. And that's one thing I gotta stop doing… all that. That's why when people go around talking about anyone's mom, I tell 'em, please don't, 'cause I don't wanna hit you. So I walk away now, I guess. Like they'll go around, they'll say: "Your mom is so ugly, she's laying around

Sheridan

the house so much." 'Cause she has depression, too, on top of HIV. They'll say: "She's too lazy, she's not even doing anything for you." I help her a lot, cleaning the house and other things. When people say that, I'm like: "You don't know how it is, 'cause you don't live with people like that."

    SHANE: Everybody else got their mothers cleaning them, make their beds, do their laundry, do the dishes, cook for them and take care of them, but we have to do that by ourselves sometimes. But once in a good while my mom will get up and cook dinner and do stuff — for us.

SHERIDAN: And, like they have fathers, too. We don't. I think he left before we were even born.

    SHANE: At home, if you said something, they'd be, like, blah blah blah, don't touch me, get away from me, leave me alone.

SHERIDAN: Or if you have a girlfriend, they'd be like: "Oh my God, you never told me your mom had it." And then they overreact, and say: "Oh my God, you have it, too. 'Cause you were born and your mom had it," and blah blah blah, and it's like: "No, I don't have it because my mom got it after we were

born." So, that's it. And then they're like: "But you still could've got it from kissing and hugging them." You're all wrong. You can't get it from hugging, you can't get it from kissing, and you can't get it from saliva.

    SHANE: In school, there's some health teachers that say: "Oh, you can get HIV from kissing someone, like spitting on them or something." I told them that it's not true. And my brother's health teacher said the same thing, that you could get it from that. But then I asked my nurse and she said you can only get it from, like, unprotected sex, blood, breast feeding, being born with it, and… open wounds. That's the same thing as blood, though.

SHERIDAN: Needles.

    SHANE: Needles. Sharing needles. And that's it.

SHERIDAN: When my mom had HIV, they were gonna try to take me and Shane away. Then, they didn't know a lot about HIV when she got it. Then they thought, Oh, we can get it

& Shane

On their 14th birthday

from her when she sits on the toilet and then we sit on the toilet, or we can get it from sharing spoons. They didn't know anything about saliva that much until they researched and researched. So my mom had to go through a lot of stuff.

    SHANE: They take you from your mother. It's like you been with your mother since she had you… Like, you been in your mother's stomach and it's a piece of her 'cause she been feeding us when she been eating, and if they take us away when we are little, it'd be taking another piece of her away, and she'd feel more tired and sick, and then she'd probably end up killing herself or something. Or dying…

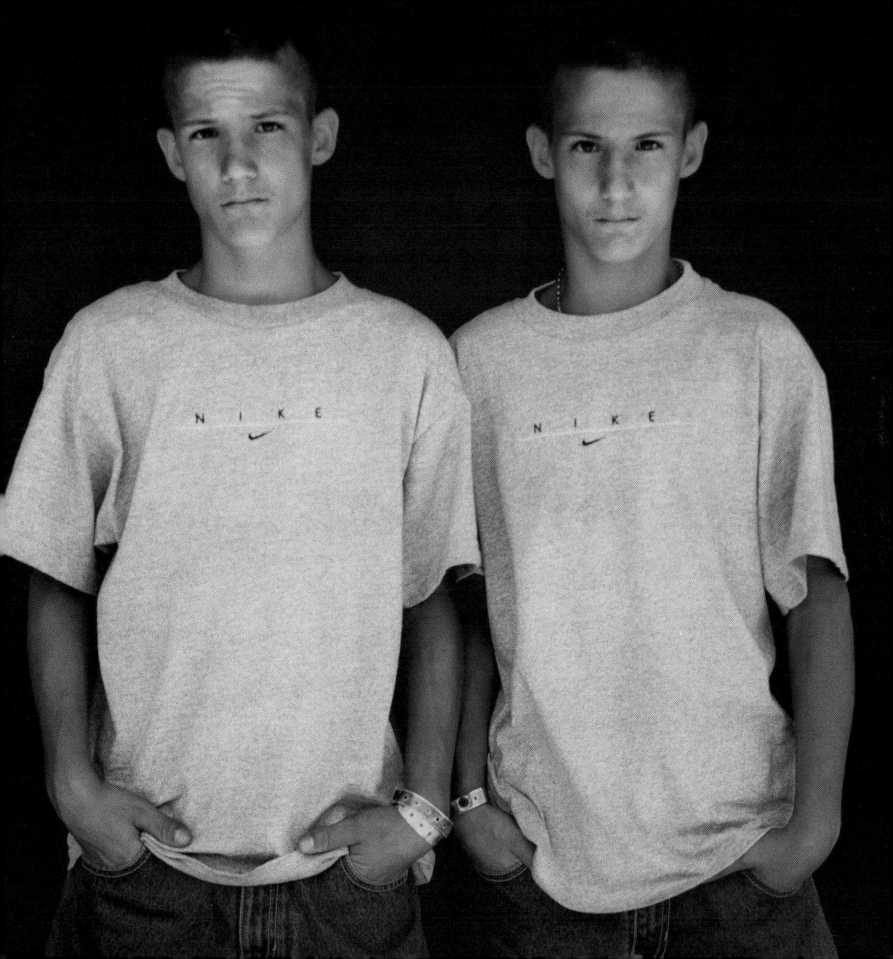

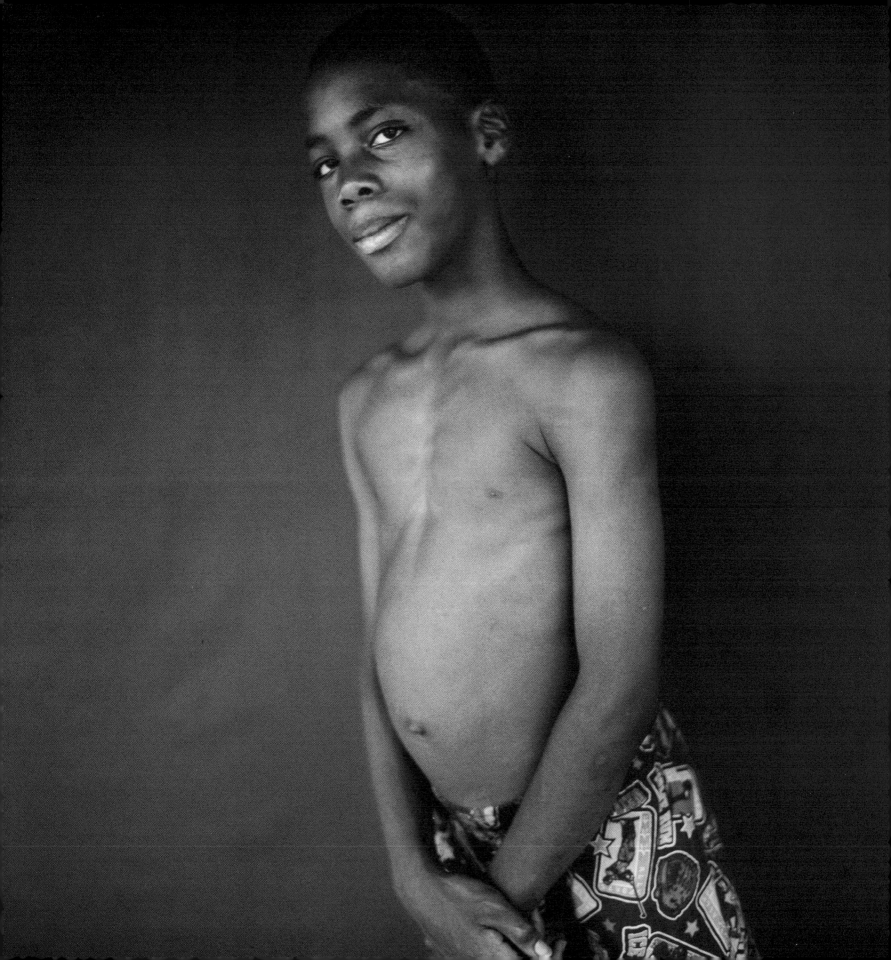

I am 12. And I have AIDS. My little baby sister, she's only 3, has AIDS. (She's not my real sister, she's my foster sister.) Nobody else in the family I live with has it, but my real parents did. I don't know if my dad has it because I'm not living with him.

I'm not supposed to tell (in school) because if they find out they'll send me somewhere else. They'll tell somebody, like the president or somebody, and he'll contact somebody and they'll send me away (to a different school) and a different family. 'Cause I can't go back to my parents. But not because of AIDS. First when I was born, I don't know why but they said my real mom threw me in a garbage can, and the police heard me crying in the can and got me out and took me to my auntie's. I don't know where my mom was, and then my auntie called somebody 'cause she was getting really sick and she couldn't take care of us anymore, my brothers and sisters anymore. We all got put in different homes, foster care. 'Cause she was really sick from AIDS, too. They sent me away to a foster home, and when I got there I didn't wanna be there.

I might get adopted if I can't go back to my real parents.

John

Age 12

I'll tell you a story. When I was in the second grade, there was a boy named Brian in my class and there was a girl named Kailey in my class, and Kailey was told by her mother that she wasn't allowed to hold my hand because I had the disease. We were going outside to play Duck-Duck-Goose one day for free time, and I wanted to be her friend 'cause she was new. I told her that I had HIV, and she told her mom that night when we went home from school.

"I don't want you hanging around that girl," her mom told her. "I don't want you holding hands or touching that girl."

And then the next day, when we played Duck-Duck-Goose, whenever I went to hold Kailey's hand to make the circle, she said, "Oh, I don't wanna touch your hand. My mom told me I can't."

And that's where one story ends. And then there's another story. The boy Brian that was also in my class, his parents were doctors, or his dad was a doctor and his mom was a nurse.

Lesley

Age 12

And what happened was, his father and his mom told Brian that HIV people and people who have full-blown AIDS, they can only live until they're 12. And so he told me that the next morning when we were walking out to PE. And I went home and I didn't know whether that was true or not, because I didn't really know about HIV and AIDS... When I was in 3rd grade, I started understanding more about HIV and AIDS, and my mom just kept on talking to me so I would understand. And so I told my mom, and she said, "Oh, well, you know people who have HIV and AIDS, they're 18 now, they're 21, they're older than 12." I still go by what she says....

I was really little and I just came out of the hospital. I was probably 7 or 8. I had an IV in my arm because they had to give me more medicine. I had been in the hospital two months and I was doing all right, and so they sent me home 'cause I was getting tired of the hospital. And then when I came home we were going to church that morning, and the pastor found out I had an IV. And there was an Easter egg hunt. And so he said he didn't want me to go to that church. My mom is HIV positive and my step dad has full-blown AIDS and so the pastor kicked us out of the church 'cause I had an IV in my hand. And it was Easter Sunday, and I really felt, I felt like I was left out. 'Cause I wanted to spend time, 'cause I had a really, really, really best friend at the church, and I haven't seen her since. I remember her name was Anna. Yeah, I remember that....

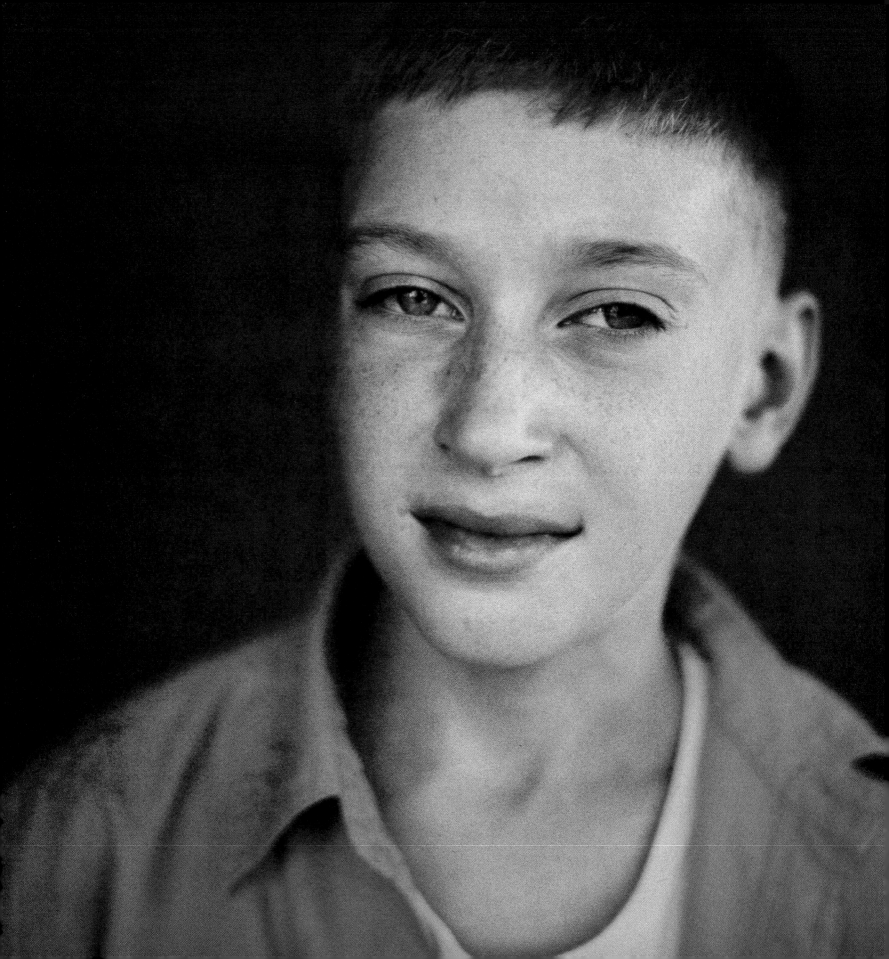

Joshua

I just turned 10 on Monday. I attend home school and I'm in the fourth grade. My favorite classes are science and history. My dream is to become an inventor, doctor or a scientist. I love to read books.

My lifelong ambition is to rid the world of prejudice. It makes me sad that I can't tell all my friends I have HIV. You never know if they will still be your friend or if their parents will let them be your friend.

I have HIV, but to tell you the truth, I forget I have it most of the time. I am reminded when I have to take all of my medicine. I take pills three times a day.

I got HIV from my mom; she got it from a blood transfusion 18 years ago. I have always known that I have HIV. My mom and dad are adopting my new baby brother. Isaiah has HIV also.

I go to the National Institute of Health in Bethesda, Maryland, for my HIV care. I have met many other kids there that have HIV. I go to Camp Heartland every summer. Camp Heartland is a place for kids with HIV. I love going to these two places because nobody is prejudiced, and I have met some very good friends there.

Ashley

Age 16

ASHLEY: My name Ashley, I'm 16.

BULINA: And I'm Bulina, I'm also 16.

ASHLEY: And we're cousins.

BULINA: Yep, we grew up together like sisters.

ASHLEY: In the "ghetto."

BULINA: And every summer's always somethin' with the girls around the corner. Because, you know, another one of our cousins, she infected with HIV. And there's always some rumors that the girls around the corner spread.

ASHLEY: So we'll go back and tell her. And let her know what people are sayin'. And sometimes she get mad.

BULINA: Sometimes she'll cry. And make us cry. But she usually just get mad. Like, there's so much anger built up for her, she doesn't think about, you know, the right way to handle things. She just, "Where they at? I'm gonna go fight now!" And then we have to fight.

ASHLEY: Fight her battles.

BULINA: For her, 'cause she's sick. She can't fight. But she'll try! She'll try, but we won't let her. Because we do it for her.

ASHLEY: Somebody'll say somethin'. They won't say it to her, they'll say it to us.

BULINA: They wanna get somethin' started.

ASHLEY: I don't know what it is. They just want somethin' started with her.

BULINA: And then they bring their aunties, you know. And the whole group, like over 20 people. They'll all come around the corner to…

ASHLEY:…our house! Like they intimidate us or somethin'. Their aunties, their friends, people that don't even know her. They come around the corner with the who-o-o-o-le neighborhood. Like, it looked like it's a thousand of them.

BULINA: And they have poles…

ASHLEY:…comin' up blastin' sticks and stuff. And they actually run on our porch and try to hit her. Which we're not gonna let happen.

BULINA: They want her to feel bad. They're very jealous.

ASHLEY: They get fulfillment. You know, when she not doin' good.

BULINA: They don't like it.

ASHLEY: When she doin' bad, they are so happy.

BULINA: They like to see theirself doin' better than somebody else.

ASHLEY: And when they see that she gettin' sick, they stop it.

BULINA: The girls who spread the rumor, they were her friends once. They were her friends and she trusted them. And she felt that she could tell 'em anything.

ASHLEY: And she told 'em. That was a stupid move.

BULINA: That was the wrong move, but... She didn't think about it.

ASHLEY: It's her doin'. She the one who brought this upon, not knowin' that it was gonna happen like this. Not knowin' it was gonna progress to this stage.

BULINA: I guess some things you just need to keep to yourself. You can't ever trust nobody but your family.

ASHLEY: She had got a boyfriend. And then the girl she told start messin' with her boyfriend. And then they got into it — and they'll be like: "The girl got AIDS!"

BULINA: He passed away.

ASHLEY: He got shot.

BULINA: Murdered.

ASHLEY: Yep. Right on our block.

BULINA: He knew that she had it, you know. But he didn't care.

ASHLEY: That's why she loved him a lot. He didn't care if she had it.

BULINA: When she was in the hospital, he went to the hospital to see her.

ASHLEY: And I liked him for that. It was like he was part of the family, instead of like her boyfriend...

BULINA: Like a cousin.

ASHLEY: Like a part of the family! When he was alive, she started gainin' her weight and stuff. And when he got killed, that's when it all went downhill. You know the thing that really really hit her? He died on our block.

BULINA: And she kinda saw. He got shot.

ASHLEY: And she lived with that memory. Every day of her life. Sometimes she'll say stupid stuff like, "I don't got no reason to live, my baby gone."

& Bulina

Age 16

BULINA: She'll just start cryin'. She still haven't forgot it.

ASHLEY: And she have crazy dreams! Crazy dreams.

BULINA: And, sometimes she can't sleep in her room. She sleep with my grandma.

ASHLEY: She used to have so much confidence, when she had friends. And she pretty, she real pretty. You would never think that she had HIV. Never in a million years.

BULINA: We're just tryin' to defend our cousin, that's all. That's our sister. You know?

ASHLEY: That's our heart. We don't want nobody, nothin' to harm her. We can't do nothin' about the HIV part, but we ain't gonna let nobody talk smack to her. Let nobody, you know, touch her. She don't want nobody to feel sorry for her. We try to treat her like she somebody normal! We know that there's somethin' that makes her stand out. You know? From the inside. So even though we know that, we don't see it! We don't see HIV. We see our cousin. We see the person we grew up with, we don't see HIV. And sometimes I'll be, like, thinkin' — does she really got it?

BULINA: It real sad because, if you think about it, over the years we deal with so much. Stop cryin'.

ASHLEY: I know that soon she gonna die. You know, if she don't, I would be so happy. She gets sick constantly. Like, she'll be healthy like one week — or one day! And the next day she sick. Sometimes I feel like I want her to give me all her burden and stuff. So I can take it on me 'cause I don't want her to feel like that no more! We try to hide our feelings to her, so we won't let her know that we hurt. 'Cause if we hurt, she gonna hurt. You know, worser.

BULINA: We like to see her laugh, so we do…

ASHLEY: …goofy stuff.

BULINA: Stupid stuff to make her laugh, and she just be laughin' so hard. Long as we just cover it up and make her feel good, we all happy. Together.

ASHLEY: Sometimes I wish I could just turn back the hands of time. To like when she didn't know. And we was just all happy and she didn't have to take medicine. No drama. I wish we would take it back to no drama. I do love her. But sometimes, she make me wanna choke her. Like, "Ooh! Shut up talkin' to me!" She been around my grandma so much, she's just bossy.

BULINA: Like a little old lady.

ASHLEY: You're right, she's old! She's an old person in a young person body.

When I was 7 years old, I found out my mother was living with HIV. She didn't wanna tell me at first, and I found out because she and her brother were getting into an argument. And my uncle screamed out, "I'm glad you have AIDS, it's gonna kill you faster!" I ran to my room and started crying. My mom had to sleep with me for months because I thought that I was gonna lose her. Every day, I just think about what's gonna happen if something were to happen to my mom. I wake up dozens of times in the middle of the night, just going to her room and making sure she okay. And it's hard to live with it.

In '94, my father passed away from full-blown AIDS. He's the one who passed it on to my mother. And she didn't find out until he was in the hospital dying. And he knew he had it, he didn't wanna tell her. He was scared that she might leave him. He was not faithful and that's how he ended up catching the virus. It's hard. Knowing that my father would do something like that and they were married for 18 years and — he never told her, never said nothing about it.

The only thing I remember was I was at a haunted house, and my aunt came to pick me up, me and my two sisters. And she said we had to go to the hospital. My father was laying there, and he was just bones. He had no meat on him and my father was a solid man, and he had like no meat on him at all, looking so sick and just like ready to go and we just started crying, and all I remember was holding his hand. And he kissed me on my cheek and he told me he loved me. And I started crying and that was it, that was the last thing I remember of him. I was 5 when he passed away.

I miss him. I do. My mom always tells me that I was his little angel, since I was the baby, but... sometimes I just have anger towards him. Like, why couldn't he tell my mom? Why? She woulda been there for him. After 18 years, he couldn't be honest with her, he couldn't stay faithful. He didn't realize that he was not only hurting himself, he was hurting his wife and his three kids — that he made. And sometimes I just wanna ask him why? Like, why did he not tell my mom and why would he do that to her if he cared about her so much? Or so he said.

The things he did were horrible. My mom deals with a lot now. She thinks about past memories and she just cries. He was abusive towards her and she thinks about that, and he was just never there, and then he... he did this to her and just left. He's not even with us no more. I believe he coulda said something to my mom and I think things woulda been different than what they are now. My family, they can't accept that my mother's livin' with HIV. Her mom barely talks to her. My uncle, the one who I found out from, he's not in our life. And from my dad's side of the family, they believe that my mother did it to *him*. So they're not in our life, and it's like basically, we just have each other. Just my mom and my two sisters and that's it. We really don't have family to depend on, and it seems like everything just fell apart.

Erica

Age 16

Rebecca

Age 12

REBECCA: I am 12 years old. My brother Brandon, he's 13. There's five of us. I'm the youngest one. He's the youngest one after me. All brothers, one sister. On Camp Heartland's Journey of Hope tour, I was talking about how I had AIDS. And I didn't feel so bad about it. 'Cause, I don't know, everybody understood that I had AIDS and they weren't "eeeww" — walking out on me and everything. They weren't doing that. Everybody understood.

BRANDON: When I tell people my sister has AIDS, sometimes they like to distance themselves. That makes me feel bad, and I tell my sister those aren't her real friends, you know. But she always has friends. The only time you have to be worried is if any blood transfer is going on. If somebody gets a cut, somebody else has an open scab and they're dealing directly with the blood, then you can worry about it. But in the meantime, don't try to be all icky about other people and try to make them feel bad. Because children with AIDS, they're like regular people. They have feelings, too.

& Brandon

Age 13

REBECCA: The only people I can trust are the people I know. My best friend, Shanna, she knows. She don't care. She's still my best friend. If you're not my friend then just don't talk to me, 'cause there's more people in the world. But people gotta get through to those people that don't know. I want to tell them, "Don't be afraid of people who have AIDS, don't fight people with it. Fight AIDS." That's it. That's the main point I wanna tell them.

BRANDON: I'd like everybody to let everybody know. 'Cause then we can separate people who are really hip to it and people who are kinda scared. So we can teach people who are kinda scared that it's all right. I think they have false ideas about like how you can get AIDS — from giving somebody a kiss or, like, being around somebody with AIDS, like it's a airborne disease, but it's not. Because if that was true, we'd all have AIDS.

I think about dying a lot, I guess.

Sometimes, if I'm not doing anything, and I'm sittin' there and all of a sudden it just come in my mind. It just come. For no reason. Don't know why. I asked my doctor that. She says, "I have no clue why. It just happens to you guys." That's what she said.

It gets harder I think. To try to cope and understand. What your body's going through, what you're goin' through, basically.

When you're little, you don't think about that. When you're little, you don't know what that means. You're like, "Oh, I'm goin' to the doctor a lot. I'm sick." And then as you get older, you learn more facts, and you think about certain stuff more often.

I distract myself. I try to sleep and… I'll try to distract my mind from thinkin' about whatever I'm thinkin' about, so I just talk on the phone or something. I just wanna get it outta my mind.

If you can have sex, have it. As long as it's safe. And as long as you tell the person, and they're like, "Okay!" Go ahead, that's what I say. 'Cause I have friends who do it. And my point of view on it is: Whatever. As long as you tell a person.

Tia

Age 14

I tell most of my friends. It's like, you don't wanna lie no more. You just wanna get it over with and tell people. It was easier to lie when I was little!

I enjoy my life. I barely get sick. My viral load is like low. So I'm doin' good. Like if you met me, you don't think I would even have it. And I'm always just — goofy. Everybody knows me as goofy, wild Tia! And friendly and loveable.

I wanna make sure that everybody understands what kids are going through, and that they look at life in a totally different way than most people do. Kids that are infected or affected by it.

Because to them, they don't have a lotta time to live. Like most of 'em think that, so then they're gonna make the most of it.

Cardell

When I was 9, my mom said: "Mommy is very, very sick. And she has to take her little medicine. So you take care of Mommy and make sure she take her medicine."

Me: "Okay, Mommy."

When I was 10, she was like: "When you were 9 I left out a little bit. Mommy has a bad, bad sore and she needs a lot of help to get rid of it."

"Okay, Mommy.

Eleven: "Mommy has a really, really bad problem."

"Okay, Mommy."

Twelve: "Mommy has a disease."

Now: "Alright, Mommy has HIV and I'm not gonna let it grow. Straight up. So there ain't gonna be any 'Okay, Mommy' no more – it's gonna be: 'Yo, you gonna live, and that's that.'"

Lost Friends and Legacies

Memories in a Red Sunset Maple

During Camp Heartland's second summer, we planted a Red Sunset Maple tree for Adam Russell, Camp Heartland's first camper to die. Adam's brother and about 15 friends silently joined me as we planted the delicate sapling in his memory.

"This will go on living for many years," I said to the group of friends. "And so will our memories of Adam."

One by one, each person said a few words, and then spread a shovel of dirt over the tree's roots. When it was Ryan Chedester's turn, he poured his root beer float into the soil around the tree, a playful and affectionate gesture.

"He was my best friend," said Ryan, tears streaming down his cheeks.

•

Later that summer, as I was returning from an emotionally draining day, I looked up into the sky. Millions of stars shone down.

I suddenly thought of my young friend Adam Russell.

"Adam," I said to the heavens. "Prove to me you're there."

A split second later, a brilliant shooting star crossed the sky.

Some would say coincidence. I would say Adam.

— NEIL

Memorial service at Camp Heartland, 2002

Phone Calls from Fola

Fola Akinyemi became a part of the Camp Heartland family in 1999.

"You don't know me," she said, walking up to me one day at camp, "but I just need to give you a hug."

We became special friends from that moment on.

Fola and I had little in common: Me, a white, Jewish American, and Fola, a black, Christian Nigerian. As we were a decade apart in age, Fola and I were also at different points in our life. I was starting a family while Fola was preparing for college. But love and friendship transcends age, race, religion and nationality.

Fola lived in Washington, D.C., in order to seek medical treatment in the United States. She was a straight-A student with a great sense of humor and a big, hearty laugh. But, living thousands of miles away from her family in Nigeria, she was often very lonely.

Camp Heartland became her second family. She longed for a community of support, and called me at our Wisconsin office nearly every day. She talked of her fears and joys and dreams for the future, about her passion for cheesecake and The Backstreet Boys. Like a younger sister, she would give me advice on everything from my hair to my wardrobe, and pepper me with questions about my new girlfriend, Adria, now my wife.

Fola loved to talk, and she loved to sing maybe even more. When we got together, she would play me her favored boy band tunes, and in turn I would play some of my favorite country songs. Once she sent me a note suggesting we use Christina Aguilera's "Reflection" as the theme song for our Journey of Hope AIDS Awareness Program.

Like my sister coming home from college on a surprise visit, Fola would show up on my doorstep in Wisconsin unannounced. For Fola, it was worth 48 hours on a Greyhound bus to be in the warm embrace of her Camp Heartland family. And for us, it was always a treat to see her smiling face....

Despite her desire to attend college and lead a normal life, Fola was hospitalized for many months with a variety of painful AIDS-related complications. In the final weeks of her life, Fola lost her ability to speak. Lori Wiener, a compassionate social worker at Fola's hospital, suggested I come visit. But she warned me that Fola would be unable to talk. This was so unlike Fola, it was hard for me to imagine. When I walked into her hospital room on my surprise visit, I did a little tap dance and song to get Fola's attention. Her grin stretched ear to ear. And even better, when I told her news of my engagement to Adria, she spoke in a tiny murmur: "I am so happy."

Tragically, her condition worsened. As she lay in the hospital, I was at Camp Heartland. I gathered about two dozen camp volunteers who had grown especially close to Fola. As campers enjoyed their dinner and sang silly camp songs in the dining hall nearby, we stood in a cramped office while I put in a call to Fola's Maryland hospital room. On the other end of the line, her friend, Joanie Gale, held the phone to Fola's ear. We knew she couldn't speak, but we believed in our hearts of hearts that she could hear us and feel our love for her. With gusto and raw emotion, we sang our Camp Heartland birthday song to Fola, like it had never been sung before.

Fola was Camp Heartland's first counselor to die from AIDS. On the day she died, July 21, 2002 — two days after her 21st birthday — I called Camp Director Dan Fox to ask him to share the news with the camp volunteers and staff. But when Dan answered the phone, I couldn't muster any words. It hurt to breathe, much less get the sound out. Finally, in a nearly inaudible voice, I said, "Fola died."

I was defeated. Given our history together, it made perfect sense that once her voice was silenced, so was mine.

What I wouldn't give today for just another phone call from Fola.

— NEIL

Fola; July 19, 1981–July 21, 2002

Best Friends, Tanya and Fola

Take a Sip of Joy

Take a sip of joy and mix it with laughter.
This is the recipe for gratitude to my friends who are still here for me.
While we live, I feel so wonderfully blessed for having such good friends.

When I think of blue, I think of the skies and the ones I've lost.
When I think of yellow, I think of flowers in bloom and the friends who are still here.
I am abundantly grateful for everything, including the good and the bad.

— FOLA

Fola, she was lucky for a while

She didn't have t-cells for a very long time. Her viral load was very high. And she was lucky she made it as long as she did. Two days after she turned 21, that's when she passed away.

And I was just so happy she made it to 21. I never had a friend like her and I probably never will again.

And I'm gonna miss her so-o-o-o much. I miss her laugh, I miss her voice, I miss her crazy self. Her Backstreet-Boys–singing N-Sync-dancing self, you know. She was my best friend in the whole world. Because you always become friends with people you connect with, obviously if you have it, too, and they have it, you have a connection. I've lost too many friends, and it's just really hard.

I haven't talked to her in so-o-o-o long because she couldn't talk, she couldn't walk, she couldn't move. She had a feeding tube, and she couldn't talk for months. There was always that hope that she would call me and curse me out for not calling her, you know. That would be so cool, but it just didn't work out.

I felt very sorry for her because she was in so much pain all the time and she couldn't tell you.

It's painful after they die if you have it too, because you think that you might end up that way. And that's hard. I saw her a month before she died, and I knew what she looked like.

I don't want to suffer. I really don't want to suffer. Because I've seen it too many times, and I don't want to put my family through it. I don't wanna put myself through it either....

I miss her already, and it hasn't been a week yet, you know what I mean?

— TANYA

The Loss

It crushes my soul, it weighs me down
The pain that has molded the deepest of frowns
It stole that in which I breathe
That in which I live.
The pain that stole my will, my wish to give.

My life was okay, all was well
Then came the phone call that drove me to hell
The death of a friend, from so many years
Words that were beyond the worst of my fears.

I wept and I mourned for four days straight
I just sat there and wept, never slept or ate
I'm sorry I blamed God, for this I still pray
But the loss cut deeper than any bullet or blade.

I watched my own tears, and felt my soul tossed
Deep in depression I heard none but my loss
The break of my heart, that shattered my soul
Death had engulfed me and swallowed me whole.

"Rest in Peace" is all I could say
The world was my mind just day after day
Words could not comfort the pain that I had
The loss just broke me, beyond the word sad.

Death had a hold that kept me in check
A death that had shattered me and made me a wreck
I was a broken down car, that never shifts gears
I returned back to school just once that whole year.

And year after year, my mind won't sway
From the thought of my loss, the death of that day.

— NILE, AGE 16
R.I.P. C.E.

A Life with Chris

Chris was the type of kid you couldn't help but be drawn to. I first became friends with him when we were both 11, back in 1998, at camp's opening session in Minnesota. He was such a mischievous little troublemaker. We would sneak out of the cabins together late at night to go to the playground.

Chris once told me that I would always be his good friend because he knew I would never make fun of him for being small. And I never really could. The boy that I knew was a GIANT — a giant whose small stature was overshadowed by his inspirational soul.

When Chris died, I didn't do anything. I didn't move, I didn't speak, I didn't even think. Time seemed to have just stopped. Slowly, gradually, I started to function again, and the only thought inside of my head was that of me trying to believe… no, comprehend that the world no longer had an individual like Chris Edwards in it.

And that was when I cried.

A storming rain was plummeting down, but the drops weren't beating outside. No, the rain was from my tears falling on my chest.

And then I stopped crying.

Not because the tears wouldn't continue, but because Chris wouldn't have wanted them to continue. My tears have now subsided, but the sorrow has not. I carry his picture with me in my wallet everywhere I go as a constant reminder of my friend and what he meant to me… and the world.

— LUKE, AGE 18
camper and counselor at Camp Heartland

A Tree Grows in Willow River

On October 12, 1999, Camp Heartland lost our wonderful friend, Chris. Moments after he died, his mother, Tisa Edwards, called with one final request: "Noodle, I want his resting place to be his favorite place" — the Camp Heartland Center. So on a brisk October day, we scattered Chris' ashes in the soil of a tree we planted in his memory. Even now, many years after his death, I sit under "Chris' Tree". It's as if he's still with us today.

— NEIL

Lesley, age 13, with Chris' memorial tree

Online with Daniel

By Neil and Daniel

During one of our 1999 summer camps in Malibu, camper Daniel Yarnell asked me to email him as soon as I returned home to Wisconsin. That request led to a weekly exchange of emails — some of which are found in the following pages. They are part of his lasting legacy. As Daniel's condition worsened, he was too ill to travel to Camp Heartland. For Daniel, our emails were his lifeline to the Camp Heartland community. For me, our emails were a reminder that none of us have the luxury of time.

DATE: Mon, 23 Aug 1999
FROM: Neil Willenson
TO: Daniel Flip
SUBJECT: HEY Noodle!

Hi noodle

i just got home a couple hours ago from camp. Can you call the lego land for me? It is in Carlsbad/California. I don't care if you tell them i have AIDS.

    write back soon
    Daniel (FLIP)

DATE: Thu, 26 Aug 1999
FROM: Neil Willenson
TO: Daniel Flip
SUBJECT: Re: HEY Daniel!

Hi Daniel!

I'm glad this email works for you... It was really great to see you at CAMP HEARTLAND. As always, I am impressed with how nice, mature, kind and courageous you are. You are a great guy and I like spending time with you.

I will call Legoland today to see if they can give you some passes... I'll let you know... soon... I'll visit your website later today.

    Take care,
    Your friend – Neil "Noodle"

DATE: Sat, 12 Sept 1999
FROM: Daniel Flip
TO: Neil Willenson
SUBJECT: Daisy!

Do you think you can send me a poster of model Daisy Fuentes? She is the model that came to camp this summer.

    write back soon
    Daniel

DATE: Wed, 15 Sep 1999
FROM: Neil Willenson
TO: Daniel Flip
SUBJECT: re: Daisy

Hey Flippy,

Daisy Fuentes? Pretty cute!!! I will ask her or her assistant to send you a poster... I'll see what I can do... Take care, my friend.

    Noodle

DATE: Wed, 15 Sept 1999
FROM: Daniel Flip
TO: Neil Willenson
SUBJECT: Thanks

thank you for asking you're a very cool man if you didn't know that

DATE: Fri, 24 Sept 1999
SUBJECT: haha
TO: Neil Willenson
FROM: Daniel Flip

i do not listen to country music it sucks you are a dork

hahahahahahahahahahahahahahahahaha-hahahhahahahahahahahahaha

what have you been doing lately i haven't been doing anything except homework and shopping for Hotwheelz .....did you know that i am going to be getting a case of hotwheelz from wisconsin soon i hope. my birthday is coming oct 10

the case of hotwheelz has 72 cars in it and it comes from the hotwheelz factory

so anyway i got to go write back soon

    daniel

DATE: Mon, 27 Sept 1999
FROM: Neil Willenson
TO: Daniel Flip
SUBJECT: re: haha

Danielle,

You get DANIELLE because you called me a dork. Garth Brooks is a musical genius!

Hotwheels? How long have you been collecting these? I have 500 campers so I can't buy them all Birthday presents, but just in case, give me a few ideas.

    thanks, Daniel. Noodle

DATE: Thu, 30 Sept 1999
FROM: Neil Willenson
TO: Daniel Flip
SUBJECT: re: howdy

Hi Flip!

Guess what? Legoland sent me a certificate for four free passes to their California theme park. We'll chat about it soon.

    Neil

DATE: **Sat, 09 Oct 1999**
FROM: **Neil Willenson**
TO: **Linda**
SUBJECT: **Hello**

Linda,

I hope you are well. You have a bright, courageous son. Daniel is a great person. I enjoy visiting with him at Camp Heartland and emailing him regularly. Also – this will seem silly – Daniel asked me to get him a poster from supermodel Daisy Fuentes. She visited camp this summer. She sent one autographed to him. Even though he is now 15, I thought I should get your permission to send this to him because she is wearing a bikini. (Nothing private showing!) If you say no, there are a number of male friends of mine who will gladly take this! Just kidding.

Thanks again for allowing Daniel to come to camp. We all are very proud to know him.

Best wishes,
Neil "Noodle" Willenson

DATE: **Fri, Oct 29 1999**
TO: **Daniel Flip**
FROM: **Neil Willenson**
SUBJECT: **re: hi**

i didn't no that chris had died
are you bumed....i am
but we have to get over it
well, any way i went to washington and that is when i found out…
email me back as soon as you can

your email friend Daniel (FLIP)

DATE: **Tue, Nov 2 1999**
SUBJECT: **re: hi**
FROM: **Neil Willenson**
TO: **Daniel Flip**

Hi Flip,

I am very, very sad about Chris. I knew him since the beginning of camp in 1993. His mom decided to bring his ashes to camp in Minnesota and we scattered and buried them in a tree we planted. He was a very funny and hyper and nice guy! Did you know him well?

Daniel, stay cool! Your amigo –
Neil/Noodle

DATE: **Tue, Nov 16 1999**
SUBJECT: **hi**
FROM: **Neil Willenson**
TO: **Daniel Flip**

"Flip," a 5 second poem by Noodle
Flip is cool
Flip is Rad
Flip is a skater punk.

DATE: **Tue, Nov 16 1999**
FROM: **Daniel Flip**
To: **Neil Willenson**
SUBJECT: **hi neil**

i dont skate anymore
i cant i am to weak now days
write back Daniel

DATE: **Thu, Nov 18 1999**
SUBJECT: **:)**
FROM: **Daniel Flip**
TO: **Neil Willenson**

a little poem:
Neil is great
Neil is awesome
Neil is da bomb

DATE: **Wed, 08 Dec 1999**
FROM: **Daniel Flip**
TO: **Neil Willenson**
SUBJECT: **:(**

hi neil i was sick last night
i had a ceesar i dont know how to spell it
i have a big rug burn on my face and also a brooose

it feels like someone beat me up

write me back or call

DATE: **Sat, 18 Dec 1999**
FROM: **Linda**
TO: **Neil Willenson**
SUBJECT: **Daniel**

Neil, Thank you very much for taking Daniel and Curtis to Legoland. Daniel sure enjoyed it. Curtis said so too. With Daniel having a seizure the Tuesday before, I was worried that he would have another one in CA. The NIH said to go ahead and let him go. I am glad that I did. Daniel has had many tests on why he has had seizures. The only answer is that the virus is in the brain. Daniel was also devastated when he found out that Chris passed away. Daniel met Chris when he was about three. Daniel found out about Chris in DC. (a friend told him.) Daniel called me right away. He said he started to shake and felt sick to his stomach...

Talk to you again.

Thank you very much for being a part of my son's life.

Linda

DATE: **Sun, 19 Dec 1999**
FROM: **Neil Willenson**
To: **Linda**
SUBJECT: **re: Daniel**

Hi Linda,

I, too, had a great time with Daniel and Curtis. It is a tribute to you how well they get along and how kind and caring Curtis is towards his little brother.

The situation with the seizures is very sad and difficult. Despite this, Daniel seems to maintain a great attitude.

I knew Chris for many years as well. I was shocked by his death because he had so much vitality and energy. His mom and dad are "hanging in there." I have attached a Memorial announcement about Chris that we distributed at the funeral.

Linda, you have three great kids. Nice job, Mom!

take care, Neil Willenson

DATE: **Tuesday, March 07, 2000**
FROM: **Daniel Flip**
TO: **Neil Willenson**
SUBJECT: **:(**

hey neil i just wanted you to tell you that i am stil in the hospital and it is boring everytime i try to sleep they either have to take blood from me or give me medicine but i have to live with it and be tired all the time now

talk to you when i feel beter to talk and write

i actually feel beter now but i dont no when i am going to check my email

Daniel

DATE: **Wednesday, March 08, 2000**
FROM: **Neil Willenson**
TO: **Daniel Flip**
SUBJECT: **re: :(**

Daniel, I know you may not get this for a while, but I am thinking about you. I hope you are feeling better. You are such a nice person. You deserve to be happy and healthy! Take care and keep in touch.

Your friend, Neil

DATE: **Tuesday, April 25, 2000**
FROM: **Daniel Flip**
TO: **Neil Willenson**

i am fine haven't been doing anything

my easter was ok. the easter bunny didnt bring me what i wanted though which was a cure but that is ok 4 now

Daniel

DATE: **Tue, 25 April 25, 2000**
FROM: **Neil Willenson**
TO: **Daniel Flip**

Hi Flippy,

I wish the Easter Bunny could provide the CURE! That would be great.

Until we get the cure, we just have to have HOPE and LOVE and keep taking Medicine! You are a great guy.

Noodle

DATE: **Wednesday, May 03, 2000**
FROM: **Daniel Flip**
TO: **Neil**
SUBJECT: **re: :)**

This is Flip-Daniel's Dad. He is having a hard time. He may take awhile to reply to his e-mail, etc. His vision with his eyes are not too good. When he tries to read he says he can't see it.

Last Wednesday he had another seizure & was in the Hospital for a couple of days. He has been alot slower in talking and thinking since then. He does enjoy the e-mails and I will start reading them to him.

I will also start helping him to reply.

Thank you, Daniel's Dad, Gerald Yarnell (Nickname Mighty)

DATE: **Friday, May 5, 2000**
FROM: **neil**
TO: **'Daniel Flip'**
SUBJECT: **re: :)**

Hi Flip, I am very sorry to hear that you have not been doing so well... I hope you feel better soon... Always remember that you are one of the nicest, kindest and coolest people around. Everyone enjoys hanging out with you. Try to smile... When you do, it makes all those around you light up too!

Keep in touch, your friend
– Noodle Neil

DATE: **June 04, 2000**
FROM: **Daniel Flip**
TO: **Neil Willenson**
SUBJECT: **Hello**

Hi Neil, This is Daniels mom, Linda. Daniel is in pretty good spirits most of the time. He is very weak and needs help getting around.

Daniel had another seizure 2 weeks ago. That one was mild. Daniel has decided to go back on AZT but to tell you the truth I don't believe that just one drug will help him. Of course, sometimes it is just a mind over matter situation. With everything going on with Daniel, I have found that it has been hard to focus. So much that I have lost my job. Thank you very much for all of the support that you and your staff have given to Daniel and my family. Talk to you later,

Linda

DATE: **June 28, 2000**
FROM: **Daniel Flip**
TO: **'Neil'**
SUBJECT: **Hi, Flip**

Neil, How have you been? So, you are in Australia? Instead of giving a koala a hug just bring one home for me. :(Do they have beanie babies there? Talk to you when you get back. I haven't had any seizures lately.

Daniel

P.S. Mom said hi.

DATE: **July 01, 2000**
FROM: **Neil**
TO: **'Daniel Flip'**
SUBJECT: **RE: Hi, Flip**

Hi Flip!

I am back from a couple of weeks in Australia. Sorry, they don't let people bring Koalas home with them. I didn't see any beanie babies :(It sounds like you are doing better. That is great news.

How is your summer so far? Anything exciting?

Keep in touch. Noodle.

DATE: **July 18, 2000**
FROM: **Linda Yarnell**
TO: **Neil**
SUBJECT: **Re: Daniel**

Hello Neil, I hope your trip was exciting. We have not been to the NIH to have those camp papers filled out. It has been real hard on Daniel. He is so weak that he cannot get up by himself and stays in the bathroom forever. Last week he had four seizures between ten pm and five am.

Now they have him taking alot of seizure meds. As a matter of fact, he may be hospitalized for about a week here so they can decrease one med while increasing another. They say that it is dangerous to do as an outpatient.

Talk to you later!
Linda

DATE: July 19, 2000
FROM: Neil
TO: Linda Yarnell
SUBJECT: RE: Daniel

Linda, this is very sad for Daniel, your family and all of us at Camp Heartland. We care about him very much. Is there anything we can do to help? If it would be possible for him to still visit camp for a couple of days in Malibu – perhaps with you or your husband – this could be arranged.

In any case, please know that you are all in our thoughts and prayers.

Please take care.
Neil

DATE: Tuesday, September 05, 2000
FROM: Neil
TO: Flip Daniel
SUBJECT: Hello

Dear Daniel,

I wanted to write to you to tell you that
a) You are a very nice person
b) You are brave
c) I was thinking about you
d) All of the above
The Answer is: d) all of the above
Final answer? Yes, final answer. You win $1,000,000

Keep in touch,
Noodle

DATE: Saturday, September 23, 2000
FROM: Linda Yarnell
TO: Neil Willenson
SUBJECT: Daniel

Neil,

I just wanted to let you know that Daniel passed away friday, Sept 22 @ 11:35 a.m. He didn't seem to be in any pain. Thank God!! We will have a memorial service this next Tuesday @ 6:00 p.m. Talk to you later.

Linda

DATE: Monday, September 25, 2000
FROM: Neil Willenson
TO: Linda Yarnell
SUBJECT: Hello

Linda,

I am very saddened by this, but am thankful he wasn't in pain. Daniel was a remarkable young man. I will remember him fondly.

I will call you later today to learn more about the arrangements.

Please take care of yourself and take comfort that many people loved and admired your son. Please share my thoughts with you husband, Curtis and Dena.

Neil

DATE: Wednesday, October 11, 2000
FROM: Neil Willenson
TO: Linda Yarnell
SUBJECT: Thinking of You

Hi Linda,

As yesterday was Daniel's birthday, I was thinking of all of you quite a bit. I hope you are doing as well as possible.

Take care and keep in touch,
Neil

DATE: Monday, October 16, 2000
FROM: Linda Yarnell
TO: Neil Willenson
SUBJECT: Re: Dena

Neil, Thank you very much for making it possible for Dena to attend camp. I know that she enjoys that plus helping others, especially kids. Also, I found a document that Daniel was preparing for a speech for Camp Heartland:

Hi, My name is Daniel, I am 15 years old. I was born with cancer. I had my kidney removed when I was two days old. When the doctors removed it, I had a transfusion. That is how I got HIV. I have to go to the NIH hospital in Bethesda, Maryland and they do alot of tests on me and give me medicine. It isn't fun living with AIDS. I have friends who died from it. (Damon, Chris) I am looking forward on living a long life.

That is all that Daniel wrote.

Talk to you later,
Linda

DATE: Thursday, October 11, 2001
FROM: Dena Yarnell
TO: Neil Willenson
SUBJECT: Hello Noodle

Hi Noodle,

How are you doing? I am so glad you called yesterday. It was nice to hear from you. Here is the poem I wrote for Daniel's birthday:

Daniel, I made you a chocolate cake today.
I can't believe it's your seventeenth birthday.
It's been one year and eighteen days since you passed away.
I wish you were here to blow out the candles on your cake.
I have a present just for you – I'll tell you what it is.
It's a small box wrapped in purple and blue – and inside is an imaginary kiss.
Since you can't be here to open it, I'll save it for you.
Someday I'll see you in heaven and that imaginary kiss will come true.
I'm wishing you a lot of peace and happiness today.
Daniel. Have a wonderful Birthday.

Well, Noodle, I will talk to you soon.
Bye. Dena

Daniel's mom, Linda Yarnell, has published a book about her son. One Last Breath *is available at www.buybooksontheweb.com.*

85

Friends

I've known a lot of kids
Who have had HIV
Some of them are gone
And then there is me
I'm scared and worried
Especially with each new shot
I don't know why they are gone
I miss my friends a lot
I often ask
Why them?
And when will my turn be?
But the answer does not come
It is not inside of me
So I learn to live each day
Anyway I can
I think of my friends in heaven as angels
And us holding hands
For one day we will be together
Although it's not my time yet
I have too much to do and say here
I'm glad for the friends I have met

— TANYA

Why is life so short?

Why is Life so short. Is it because I have HIV/AIDS or is it because everyone dies. Everyone dies for a reason, but some times I don't understand why God takes people away from me. I wish life was not short. Life is short on earth, but eterenal in Heaven.

By Britani

POEM by
Britani, age 13

Transformations

Billy: Sick of Being Sick

At camp late one summer evening, in Cabin #6, Billy refused to take his medications. The endless routine of medications and the unpleasant side effects had gradually worn away his spirit. Although Billy knew the importance of his meds, after seven years of living with HIV he was quite literally "sick and tired of being sick and tired."

His camp counselor, Rod, stood at his bunk.

"Is there anything we can do to help you take your meds?" Rod asked. Silence followed, and in that silence Billy's weariness hung heavily in the room, for every camper there knew that weariness firsthand.

Finally, we saw Billy look up. "I'll take my meds if all of the campers hold my hand."

Without hesitation, the seven other campers jumped off their bunk beds and gathered around Billy in a circle of love and support. By embracing Billy and holding his hand, he took his meds that night… and for the rest of the week.

It's part of the magic of Camp Heartland: A burden shared can become a burden removed.

— NEIL

that is what I am so *cposed* me for me.

The Girl with the Nappy Hair

By Coral Popowitz

She was only four years old, her mother had just died, she was in a strange home with strange people, her chin never left her chest, big, brown eyes looking down, barely speaking, grieving, sad and lonely… until it came time to fix her hair. Then she spoke, told you what she needed, how her hair had to be done in braids, checked your compliance and gave you a slight smile — if you'd done it right.

Having an African American father and a Caucasian mother gave her incredibly curly, soft brown hair. Her mother had let it grow to nearly her waist, and it was stunning, the envy of any shampoo company marketer. But somewhere, someone had told her she had "nappy, nasty hair" and she believed it, so much so that every day she wanted it braided tight, all the way down, until only a slight curl made a backwards letter "C" on her back. She inspected your work, making sure every stray hair was tucked in, no "nappies" sticking out. If there were, her eyes turned sad and you instantly knew it had to be done over.

To comfort her in her grief, to bond with her, but mostly

Tiff, age 7 with her sister Mariah

not to see those sad eyes, I braided her hair everyday, and every time she inspected it. Most days I got it right. Slowly the veil of grief lifted, the bond between us grew, and the sad eyes were rarely seen… But the hair had to be braided just right, tight, with no nappies, every day, braids, every day, just right, no nappies, no nappies.

When she was six she went to Camp Heartland. There, they promised acceptance, hope, but most of all fun. There, she would meet other children who had HIV, other children that had her skin color, other children with braids and nappy hair. So we packed her bags and her medications, and most importantly to her, we packed her hair ties, brush and comb. I promised her I would teach her camp counselor how to braid her hair, how to tuck in the nappies. But as we traveled to camp, I'm not sure who had sadder eyes, she or me.

The welcoming song and clapping scared her and she started to cry… Me too, but I didn't let her see. Instead we walked up to her counselor and I took out the bag of hair ties and explained how important it was to have her hair braided each day and the

Tiff, age 8

to something funny, and her hair … was one-big-puffy, flowing-in-the-breeze, brown mass of curls that hadn't seen a hair tie or a brush and comb in days!

Tiff was free. You could see it in her face and in her hair. The nappies were everywhere… And it was okay. In her first short stay at Camp Heartland, she had found more than friendship and fun, she found other kids, other little girls and adults who had HIV, too. She had found other little girls who had brothers and sisters that didn't have HIV, just like her. And she had found friends whose moms had died, too.

What I saw in that big, beautiful Afro surrounding her smiling face was acceptance. The girl with the nappy hair had found acceptance… of herself.

My Name is Tiff

Hi, my name is Tiff — would you like me if…
I liked Justin Timberlake and Britney Spears?
If I like 'N-Sync and my age is only nine years?

My name is Tiff, would you like me if…
I liked monkeys and sponges and Rugrats?
If I like Winnie the Pooh and Minnie Mouse
But I liked Eeyore more?

My name is Tiff, would you like me if…
I had brown eyes and brown skin?
If my hair is sometimes nappy? (That makes me unhappy.)

My name is Tiff, would you like me if…
I was adopted and my family is white?
If I had a million friends? (Well, not quite.)

My name is Tiff, would you like me if…
I had to take 14 pills every day?
If sometimes I get sick and then in the hospital I stay?

My name is Tiff, would you like me if…
My mom died of AIDS disease and I have HIV?

Would you like me, hug me or be my friend…
Please?

— TIFF

nappies tucked in, just right. We finished checking in and, slowly and hesitantly, I walked away as my tiny little 6-year-old adopted daughter held the hand of another adult for the first time in two years and walked away from me, chin to chest.

For two days I worried and wondered if things were going well. I knew she'd get her meds, I hoped she'd make friends, and I was confident in the counselor's braiding ability. But still I worried about how she was doing. I kept seeing her sad, lonely eyes until, finally, on the third day, I had to see for myself. I went back to Camp Heartland, I made my way stealthily onto the campsite and, to the first adult I saw, I frantically explained my angst and begged to check on her, promising not to let her see me.

As I scanned the campsite, I saw a group of young boys doing silly dances, older girls chattering away as they hung tie-dyed t-shirts on the clothes line. A game of kickball was in full swing… Where was she? Scanning again I could hear the uninhibited laughter, see the huge smiles, feel the fun and excitement.

Then I saw her. She was on the picnic table with a group of girls looking at nature finds. Her chin was not on her chest, she was looking up, toward the sun, there were no sad eyes, her eyes sparkled, her full lips turned up in a smile as she listened

Every Camp Heartland child leaves an indelible impression on Camp Heartland's counselors and staff members. Two of our earliest staff members, Susan Leckey and Janet Osherow, have fond memories of hundreds of campers, but one girl in particular has forever touched their hearts.

I first met Lupe when she was 11. She didn't speak much English and she didn't seem very healthy most of the time. But she was always happy and spread her cheerfulness all around camp. If anyone was down she'd say "Don't cry. It's okay," in her sweet, Mexican accent.

One day, when Lupe was 16, her sister, Karina, sent me an email: "Lupe is in the hospital. She has an infection in her body." I called the hospital and, in my broken Spanish, spoke to her mother, Santos. She was crying. *"Es muy mal,"* she said. *"Muy mal"* — very bad, very bad. The next morning, the doctors said Lupe might not make it much longer. I got in my car at 5 in the morning and drove 350 miles from Milwaukee to the Minneapolis hospital as fast as I could.

Lupe

Te quiero mucho

Lupe was in a coma with dozens of tubes sticking out of her. Many of us from Camp Heartland were at her side, making promises to Lupe if she would just come out of the coma. And I told Lupe that I would take her to Disneyworld if she woke up.

But it didn't look good…

Well… Disneyworld was a BLAST! We rented a convertible, got soaked in a rain storm, bought Mickey Mouse rain ponchos, rode all the scary rides and did the whole park proud.

Lupe continues to amaze and inspire us all. She may be small in size but not in her will to live. Today, she speaks publicly about her struggles and her dreams. She is my hero.

As we always say, *Te quiero mucho*.

— JANET OSHEROW

I met Lupe in 1997 and was struck by how gentle and happy she was, even though she spent more time in the hospital than out because of her AIDS complications. She seemed to accept that this was her life and she needed to make the most of it.

Still, the virus was taking hold of her body. On one occasion, her kidneys shut down and she slipped into unconsciousness. Her physicians told us her chance of survival was slim to none.

As the days turned into a week and then two, we all wondered how this small body could still go on fighting. Our bedside vigils were daily.

Then, one day, Lupe suddenly woke up. All she could think about was that she had just received her application to become a Camp Heartland staff member and needed to wake up so she could turn it in on time. She had waited years to become a camp counselor and was not going to let anything stop her….not even a coma!

Despite ongoing medical procedures, including 15 hours of dialysis each week, Lupe graduated from high school and is now in college. And, yes, when she has "spare time," she is on the camp's staff.

Mi Corazón

Lupe believes that she is alive today because of the support of her family and Camp Heartland. I know this is true, but Lupe is also alive because of her own inner strength and sense of purpose.

Through her laughter and hopefulness, she is a role model and inspiration. I know *mi corazón* will always be much fuller because of my friendship with Lupe.

— SUSAN LECKEY

Camp is my life.

Since the first day I heard of it. My sisters had the chance to enjoy and feel free to express their feelings about me. It was scary for them and for me, too. I didn't know anything about this topic, until I went to camp. In school, too. At camp I noticed I wasn't the only one with the virus. Every time I'm here at camp, I feel at home. At Camp Heartland I can talk about the virus.

Thanks to camp, I'm here today. Last year, I reached the end and almost died, but thanks to camp and my family, I didn't open the door to heaven. Instead I turned over and thought... *I want to be a staff member at Camp Heartland.* If I open that door now, I'll never reach my goal. I won't open the door to heaven until I reach *all* my goals.

P.S. Camp is not just a fun place but is an inspiration to all those who live with HIV and AIDS.

**LOVE, LUPE / "SURVIVOR"
JULY 2002, AGE 17**

Lupe

95

My name is Lisel, Head Camp Assistant and former camper at Camp Heartland. I've been involved with Camp Heartland since I was 15 years old. Camp Heartland has become my main support system since that first camp session and has been the reason for my transformation from a shy teenager to a confident young woman.

Even though I was born with HIV, I was not told of my diagnosis until I was 12 years old. From that moment on, I felt like I was in a downward spiral. Growing up HIV positive and feeling like there was no one else who understood me or what I was going through caused me to experience severe depression. I withdrew entirely from friends, family and my school community.

A school counselor told me about Camp Heartland and recommended that I give this program a try. She thought it was vital for me to meet other young people who were in the same situation as I was. While I was hesitant about meeting new people and sharing my personal darkness and medical issues with them, Camp Heartland opened up a whole new world to me. Over and over again, they demonstrated to me that people love me despite my disease, and that I wasn't alone. For the first time in my life I felt totally accepted. Thanks to Camp Heartland programs, a dedicated staff and my own hard work, I have become an accomplished public advocate and speaker at HIV and AIDS conferences and hearings nationwide. I am heavily involved in planning and staffing summer camping programs as well as outreach and support initiatives on a year-round basis.

Lisel

to Counselors

Shakia

My brothers and I attended our first session at Camp Heartland in 1997. It was my first time at camp and I didn't know very many people. But my brothers had been to camp before, so it wasn't long before they ditched me to play with their friends. Soon a group of counselors approached me. They seemed genuinely happy to see me, like they had known me for years. They introduced me to all of my cabin mates, and everyone seemed to hit it off right away. We were the oldest kids in camp — a group now known as the "APs," which stands for Adventure Program.

Our group grew close. We made up chants and songs for the APs and did lots of things that I never thought I would do, like caving, rope courses and "canafting" — a mix between canoeing and rafting. Our counselors kept telling us "to step outside of our comfort zone." Everything we did was a challenge, and our counselors were right behind us. They encouraged us to support and trust each other... lessons of encouragement that still help me take on new challenges to this

day. Their love and support made Camp Heartland a permanent part of me — just in that first week! There was no way that I wasn't coming back.

I returned the next year as a Junior Counselor. There was a big difference. Even though my responsibilities as a JC kept me from hanging out with my friends from the previous summer, I really loved the campers. As a camper, I had thought it was so weird that the staff walked around hugging everybody for no reason. Now, being a counselor, I can never give enough hugs and love. The greatest feeling is knowing I have touched a child's life... that I've been part of what is probably the best week of their life. My favorite part of returning to camp each year is seeing my campers from the last year run up to me wanting to know if they are in my cabin again.

Camp Heartland is like a cycle of love. It is hugs and kisses, singing and dancing, laughter and crying, joy and pain, hope and acceptance, support and celebration. And finally — as the camp song goes — it is "happiness in a circular motion."

To help shape the future for young people living with HIV and AIDS, Lisel and Shakia serve on the Camp Heartland Board of Directors.

OPPOSITE LEFT: Lisel, summer 2002
ABOVE: Shakia with Diamond, 2002

Hug-a-Bug

It's not everyday that you get to see a 5-foot tall bumblebee…

My mom is a talented, intelligent and caring woman. Yet, like so many others, she was misinformed about HIV/AIDS. As a result she was wary of my friendship with Dawn Wolff and her son, Nile — both of whom where living with AIDS. Case in point: when Dawn baked an apple pie for my family, my mother refused to eat any of it, fearing that somehow she would be at risk for getting HIV.

With that fear in mind, she was dubious of my plans to start a camp for children with the disease. As I shared with her my dream of founding Camp Heartland, with a smile on her face she proclaimed, "Get a job, Neil" — but she was only half joking.

Even though I told her that HIV could not be transmitted casually, she worried that I would somehow be the "one in a million" who became infected. I knew from medical evidence that there was no "one in a million." Simply put, I would not get HIV from becoming friends with those who had acquired the virus.

Although my mom felt great sympathy for Dawn and Nile, this was 1991, and most people at that time were fearful of those with AIDS. Still, it was frustrating that my own mom was afraid as well.

Today, Barbara Willenson couldn't be any more supportive and loving of our campers. Nearly every summer at Camp Heartland, she dons a black-and-yellow bee costume and a pair of antennae, and becomes "the Hug-a-Bug," handing out treats to campers of all ages.

"Would you like to hug the Hug-a-Bug?" she asks as she makes the rounds at camp. And after a big squeeze from a little boy or girl, she'll reach into a shopping bag for a package of juju bears.

I think her transformation can be traced to her visit to the opening day of Camp Heartland's inaugural session in 1993. With tears in her eyes she said, "There is so much love here. I have never experienced anything like it before." By meeting the actual campers themselves, it was second nature for my loving mother to open her arms and heart to these kids. By literally connecting with the children, my mom finally believed the facts that HIV is not transmitted casually.

It is inspiring to realize that a woman who was once afraid to hug any child with AIDS is now hugging hundreds of children with AIDS. Her evolution — from skeptical bystander to a champion of all people with AIDS — illustrates the power of both compassion and HIV education efforts.

Thanks, Hug-a Bug — errrr, Mom.

— NEIL

Camp Spirit

At the end of each session, as often as possible, I try to accompany the campers to the airport for a personal send-off.

This year, the departing campers brought a little bit of camp spirit to Minneapolis-St. Paul International Airport.

As we marched down the long concourse on our way to our gate — lugging suitcases and lifting backpacks and snacking on peanut butter sandwiches — the kids began to get a little restless. To kill the time as they rode the moving sidewalks, they began to sing:

"Hey Noodle!"

"Hey what?"

"Shake your bootie!"

"No way!"

"Shake your bootie!"

"Okay…"

"Jump! Shake your bootie"

"Jump, Jump! Shake your bootie…"

As we passed the traveling business executives, I watched the expressions on their faces turn from annoyance to amusement to delight. I think I might even have heard one singing along.

— NEIL

Daniella

Escaping from AIDS
By Janet Osherow

DRAWING by Chanel, age 10

It was early summer, 1994. I was helping with camp registration and making phone calls to parents before the upcoming session in August. One particularly anxious mom told me her 11-year-old daughter, Daniella, was nervous and didn't want to come. So, in the weeks before camp, I started calling Daniella on a regular basis, trying to help ease her anxiety and get her excited about the camp activities.

"As soon as you arrive at camp, come and find me," I told her. "I'll be your first friend."

August arrived, and on the first day of camp, a counselor came up to me and said, "There's an adorable little girl who says she's looking for her friend, Janet Planet."

Daniella had a great time that year and made a lot of friends. But shortly after camp that summer, her mother died after a long battle with AIDS. Daniella and I tried to stay in touch, but she moved from foster home to foster home, and it was hard for me to find her. I often wondered if I should adopt her or become her foster mother myself, even though I wasn't that much older than she was. Unfortunately, so many of our kids have had rough lives at home, and I certainly couldn't take them all in.

I had helped Neil start the camp in 1993. But in December of 2003, after 10 years with Camp Heartland, I made the difficult decision to leave in order to pursue a Master Degree in Social Work. A few months after I left, I was thinking about Daniella and wondered how she was doing. I hadn't heard from her in a while. Then out of the blue — it could have been the very same day — I get an email from the Camp Heartland office saying Daniella had called and was looking for me. I called her immediately. We've remained in touch the best we can.

Daniella is now 22 years old. During a recent phone conver-sation, she shared her entire life history. I knew some of it, but never realized how tough things once were for her. In her short life. she lost both of her parents to AIDS, moved to a number of foster homes, lived with a drug-addicted sister and, during her teen years, turned to drugs herself. She had thoughts of suicide and dropped out of high school. But at the age of 19, she finally realized she was wasting her life.

"If I don't get my high school diploma and clean myself up, I'm not going to be anybody," she told herself. Courageously, she returned to high school and got her diploma. She now goes to college in Vermont and is working full time on campus. She is also engaged.

"As bad as everything got, as much as I've been through, I wouldn't changed anything," Daniella said to me one day, "because I know it happened for a reason. It brought me to Camp Heartland, and you were always there for me. You have no idea how much you have helped me through the years. Camp was my escape from AIDS and from my sister doing drugs. I just want to thank you for everything you've done for me."

Thinking of her words — that we had made an impact on her life — I can only hope that she knows how much of an impact she and all of the kids and staff of Camp Heartland have made on our lives... and continue to make, each and every day.

Mark

"Doing the Best with What I've Got"

My age is 24 and I was born a hemophiliac with clubfeet. I have Hemophilia A, Factor VIII deficiency. I also have Hepatitis C and AIDS.

Would you call me crazy if I said I have gained more than I have lost by having these diseases? I ask you this because I am looking for the answer myself…

During the summer before seventh grade, my brother wanted his friend to sleep over one night and my father said no because there was something my parents wanted to talk to us about. At first I thought, "Oh great, here comes the sex talk." I was lying on the couch and my father came into the living room and sat down by my feet at the end of the couch. My mother soon followed, sitting in a chair next to my dad. They called in my brother and turned off the TV. There wasn't any beating around the bush.

"Mark," said my father, looking me in the eyes. "You're HIV positive."

At this time, most people, let alone young kids, didn't know what HIV actually was. So it didn't really hit me right away. I just stared back at my father. I then looked at my mother and she was crying. I looked over at my brother sitting on the floor across the room and he was crying, too. The same brother who I would always fight with, crying. Then I looked back at my dad and he was even crying. Except for the time my grandfather passed away, this was the only time I had seen my father cry, so I knew this

Mark on Christmas morning

was serious. This is when I started to cry, and I couldn't stop. I cried so much that I started to gag. I cried and cried and finally went into the bathroom and threw up.

My family was there for me, but I couldn't help but feel alone. Instantly, at the age of 13, I became a person I never knew I was. It's almost as if, for your whole life, you think you are an amazing singer, and then one day you begin to sing and it sounds horrible and the audience walks out on you. You are left standing there on stage, all alone.

After finding out I was HIV positive, I was forced to make a decision about whether or not to "go public." My parents told me it was up to me and they would back me with whatever I decided. I heard a lot of stories that weren't so appealing to people with HIV. Thinking back to before I found out I was positive, I remember my mom having all these magazines with Ryan White on the cover. I remember my parents telling me we all had to sit down as a family to watch an after-school special with Magic Johnson answering questions. As a fifth grader, I would never have imagined why. And then there were the other stories, like Joey DiPaolo, someone who ended up becoming a good friend of mine, who was kicked out of school in New York. And there was the Ray family in Florida, whose house was fire-bombed. So after hearing these stories, I decided to not to tell anyone.

Keeping this secret was awful. But thank God for camp! Boy, was I nervous going for the first time. I attend four different camps, including Camp Heartland and The Hole in the Wall Gang Camp, Paul Newman's camp in Connecticut for children with chronic illnesses. I was a pretty shy kid, so being dropped off all by myself in a strange place was very intimidating… at first. After a couple of days I learned what camp was all about: Camp is full of love and acceptance. I was able to open up for the first time in years. It was the only time I felt free, free to be myself and free to express myself.

There is an unconditional bond between all the campers, because everyone is going through what you are going through. At home, my parents were the only people I could talk to. At camp, there were hundreds of people to talk to, kids in your cabin, older kids, counselors, and administrators. And if you felt comfortable enough, you could talk to younger kids and try to help them with problems you may have already worked through.

Camp taught me that it's okay to be myself, to never give up, to keep living your life no matter what walls are blocking your path, to care for one another even if you had never met before. And most importantly, it showed me that there are good people out there, people who care. I was so scared to talk about my medical conditions because of all the negative stories I heard. Well, now I see positive stories, starring positive people. This is what gave me the confidence to start telling people outside of camp, and allowing them into my life. These camps provide a place for children from all over the country where they are no longer kids with AIDS or kids with hemophilia or kids with cancer. For this one week, they can finally just be kids.

After attending camp for a few years as a camper, I realized a good way to give back and to help children was to become a counselor myself. Kids like to know other people are going through what they're going through, and they have this enormous amount of trust in you if you open up to them — if

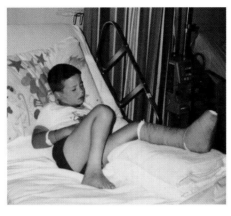

TOP: Mark, 1987
BELOW: Mark with his dad, Stephen, before Senior Prom, 1998

they believe you. I once was a counselor for a little boy who had AIDS. I opened up and told him I was also infected with HIV. He looked up at me with is eyes wide open and a smile on his face.

"No, sir, you're lying. You're just saying that," he said to me.

"Why would I just say that?" I replied.

Well, the moral of the story is, once I convinced the boy I wasn't lying he opened up to me and we became great friends.

To think that I may have helped him makes proving to him I had HIV worth every second. It's funny because outside of camp I had to lie about not having HIV. And at camp I had to prove I wasn't lying about having HIV.

I started giving speeches all over the country — to high schools, colleges and youth groups. I talked about camp, AIDS and hemophilia. The reception I would receive after a speech was very overwhelming, in a good way. College students would come up to me crying, telling me about their loved ones, or maybe how I changed them.

I remember speaking at a fundraiser with Billy Ray Cyrus, the great "Achy Breaky Heart" country singer; he had to follow me and sing his song. He told me after the event that when he was called up to the stage he was caught off guard. He wasn't ready to go on and really didn't want to follow me. I'm not a great speaker, I just speak from the heart, and that's what people listen to.

Except for people at camp, I didn't tell anyone I had HIV or even that I was a hemophiliac until I got to college and had three roommates. My plan was to take my meds right in front of them, and when they would ask what the medicine was for, I would tell them I have HIV. Simple as that.

About a month went by and … nothing! Then, finally, it happened. I was taking my medicines one day, and the dorm room was full of kids from all around our hall. One kid asked what my pills were for. I looked around and saw everyone looking at me. Quickly my brain went into hyperspeed.

Is now the time? I asked myself.

No, not now. Everyone is here, I thought.

Just do it, said another part of me.

I can't. But it was time to step up. There is never a right time. So I took a deep breath and said to the guy, "HIV. I'm HIV positive."

He looked at me for a second and said, "That sucks, man. I'm sorry."

I was free. That was it, I did what I was never able to do before and just had to hope they could accept it.

And they did. Almost everyone who was in that room on that day are still my best friends – over six years later. It's the greatest thing in the world.

This gave me the confidence to start slowly telling some friends back home. The reaction was the same. Still, I have very close friends who I just haven't told yet. It's not the easiest thing to bring up. No matter how many times I tell myself there is no *right time* to tell them, it never seems to be, well, the right time.

As I was graduating from high school, I found out I also had contracted Hepatitis C. I got C from my blood-clotting Factor for my hemophilia. There I was, at the age of 18, already facing the possibility of getting cirrhosis of the liver. This hit me hard at first because, to me, it was another thing on my plate, a kick while I was down: Oh yeah, no big deal, just another life-threatening disease. Hemophilia, HIV, Hepatitis C… What's next?

A couple years after I found out I had Hepatitis C, I was again about to hear something new. I was seeing my immunologist every other month or so. And it was at one of these visits that he gave me the news. "The last blood test showed that you now have AIDS." Full-blown AIDS.

I'm not sure I can explain why this term upsets me. Let me say that this doesn't really change anything besides the wording. The only difference between HIV and AIDS (to me, at least) is that it shows the state the virus is in, which means the state your body is in. If you have full-blown AIDS, you are more susceptible to illnesses and opportunistic infections than if you have HIV. When I have my blood work done, there are two main things they look at, my viral load (how much of the virus is in my blood) and my T4 cell count (white blood cells that are vital for your immune system). At the time I was first given the news, my viral load was "undetectable." This does not mean I am cured, it just means there is so little virus in the blood it is undetectable by the tests they use, but it is still in my body. The main determination between HIV and AIDS is when your T4 cell count drops under 200, it is then you have AIDS.

The Journey

I was asked to go
To talk
To save lives
So should I go?
I stopped and thought about it
I couldn't say no
Because I knew what was right
So I took my flight
The moment I landed
I dropped my shield
I was myself complete
No more secrets
Secrets, oh man, secrets
Stop the lies, no more lies
No backing up now

It was do or die
The words were excited
Anxious, scared
How will I be treated?
That is the one thing I feared
It was my turn
I had to step up
One way or another
I had to learn
I said my words
Finally I said my words
I looked out
I saw me out there
My age
My body

They didn't laugh
Make fun
They clapped
My heart grew, opened up
It was done
I was getting all these hugs
It was all just so fun
And it was done
WAIT
Hey, it's DONE
I'm back in the air
My shield is back up
To open up again, I don't dare
Back to the same fear
I hate to hide

Break out
I'm stuck
I can't bear it
This bubble must pop
My candle can't be lit
The people are the wind
Blowing me out
I want to keep trying
But I find myself lying
And I keep dying
Someday I will be free
No insecurity, no fears
I will just give love,
Feel love, and be happy.

— MARK

Does this change anything for me? No. I disagree with the system of categorizing the virus. It doesn't make sense. I *feel* no different and I *am* no different, I just now have AIDS.

As far as my medicines… I take quite a bit. I find it is a lot easier if I take my medicine as part of a routine. It used to be, I would never take my Factor when I should have. I would just put it off until *I had time.* So I would often go untreated. Now that I am on prophylaxis – having to infuse myself every other day no matter *what* — it makes me stick to the regimen. It is the same with my other meds.

So as you can see, I'm not exactly what you would call *healthy*. But one good thing that came out of all this medical mayhem is that I am even more appreciative of life. I always say: Live everyday like it's your only day, treat everyone better than you want to be treated and keep smiling through it all. Having three life-threatening diseases has led me to think and act a little differently than the average person. I will never sit inside playing video games all day. I love experiencing new things. Knowing how little time we have in this world and how much there is to see in this world, how can I possible sit still? I have lived in Massachusetts, I went to college in Connecticut, and worked as an environmentalist in Hollywood. I interned for MTV and VH1 in Times Square, back-packed Europe for two months, deejayed at a rock station in NYC, and started my own video production company. So, if you can find time in there for sitting around and letting life pass by, please let me know so I can fix that.

When any man or woman in this world is faced with a challenge, he or she has two choices: give up or step up. That's not as easy as its sounds. Even if you choose to step up, the road ahead will never be a smooth and straight path. There are times you will have to remind yourself which choice you made and why you made that choice. Even though there are times I may tell you I chose the first option, to give up, I always remember why I prefer the second option more. It's simple: my parents, my brother, my niece, my whole family, my best friends, my party friends, my laid back friends, my co-workers, my teachers of life and all the people I will always love. It is for you I choose to step up. It's hard, but at the end of the day, it is worth it.

So have I gained more than I have lost? I still don't know. I have lost my health, the ability to play sports, the memories of what it's like to not feel sick and tired, the ability to straighten my arms, the freedom to go somewhere without having to bring my medicine, and possibly the opportunity to live a long life. And what have I gained? I've gained knowledge. I know that even though I may not have the quantity of days I wish I had, I do have control over the quality of my days. I have gained appreciation of the world around me, and how beautiful this planet can be. I have gained experiences, of going to camps all over the country and giving speeches to dozens of colleges, and gaining friends along the way.

But most importantly, I have learned to be myself, and how to make myself better. When I become a better person, the people around me become better people, and then the people around them become better people, and on and on.

So have I gained more than I have lost? Maybe there's not an answer for that. I do know, no matter what that answer is, I'm going to do the best I can with what I've got.

Mark (right), Switzerland 2002

Obstacle

As people get sicker
Most people feel the need to whisper
About what they have,
A sickness which has been discriminated against.

But, here at camp, it's fun, safe and you can be open.
Our mind, feelings and sense of communication
Is no longer fenced.

Talking, laughing, crying, sharing
All with people who are the same or not
You've shown that you do not
Have to walk around with shame.

You become proud, confident
And more proud about who you are,
And you learn to show people that you are
A human being like everyone else.

Love yourself like I do
Be confident,
Live life, no matter what problems are
Put in front of you.

Life is an obstacle course,
Race yourself and finish first.

— WILL, AGE 16
Camp LIT, "Leader in Training"

Course

Heroes

The Power of You

From the pages of this book, I hope you have gained some understanding of the many issues that children affected by HIV/AIDS face on a daily basis.

It is difficult to imagine a group who suffers more than children with HIV/AIDS. Not only do they face the ravages of the disease with ongoing illnesses, but they also must endure fistfuls of distasteful medicines and their horrible side effects, painful medical procedures, grief for loved ones lost, and the fear of their own mortality.

A Call To Action

Coupled with the discrimination, paranoia and stigma still associated with HIV/AIDS, it is clear that children afflicted with the disease often lead sad and lonely lives. With that in mind, Camp Heartland's medical, social work, and camping professionals work throughout the year to give these children unconditional love and acceptance.

On the following pages, you will find stories about a few of the many "Heartland Heroes" who have changed the lives of Camp Heartland's children. At the end of this section you will find answers to "Frequently Asked Questions" about HIV/AIDS, the Journey of Hope Awareness Program and the camp itself.

— NEIL

Eric, age 13

Camp Counselors

THE HEARTBEAT

The counselors and staff of Camp Heartland are some of the most giving people around. Some have quit jobs, canceled vacations or even postponed school plans to put in time at camp. Some have known people with AIDS. One young counselor lost her older brother to the virus. Another is recovering from cancer. A handful of counselors are HIV-positive themselves.

At day's end — after 15 hours cast in the roles of parent, older sibling, coach, art teacher, therapist and friend to dozens of kids — our camp counselors need a break. If they're not on duty, you can find them sitting around the staff lounge, sharing pizza and Diet Coke, laughing, crying — sharing awe-inspiring stories of courage and compassion and love, stories that quite literally have changed their lives.

Kara with Timothy, age 12

Kara Chitwood
served in many staff positions for Camp Heartland.
She's now an education programs assistant for Camp Heartland.

I was at camp for a mini-session — four days, 40 kids, less intense than a normal summer session. And in every session at camp, there's always "that kid" — the child that everyone wants to take home. This weekend, "that kid" was an 8-year-old African American girl named "Rebecca." She's cute as a button, always smiling, loves sitting on laps, is grateful for camp food. (When we were served chicken and dumplings for dinner one evening, she commented that "at least we have food, because not all people do.") Rebecca, a pretty darned-good reader for a second grader, is HIV positive.

I happened to be in Club Meds, our nurses station, and the place where staff go to get chocolate (oops, I mean our own "medicine") and Rebecca was taking her meds. She was sitting with nurse Peggy, working up to taking her Kaletra, the nastiest of the nastiest tasting liquid medicines ever created. Rebecca throws up every time she takes it, and has to re-take it a few times to make sure it stays down. It tugged — no, yanked — on my heartstrings to see this child fuss and put her beautiful little face in her arms in attempt to evade the inevitable.

She took her meds and threw up.

But the next day, I saw Rebecca in Club Meds again. She was taking another round of meds with Peggy, and I sat next to her as she put a plastic syringe in her mouth and shot in some mildly bad tasting medicine.

"Hey Kara?" she said. "Hey what?" I answered.

"Guess what I did today?" And yes, folks, Rebecca did it! She took her Kaletra without throwing up! Her big brown eyes were sparkling and she was just a-smilin' away!

Dr. Andrea Hoogerland and counselor Ryan help Timothy, age 9.

Janet Osherow

was a counselor and executive at Heartland from 1993-2003. She is now pursuing a Masters Degree in Social Work. When she graduates, she plans to continue working with at-risk youth.

It was the first day of camp in the summer of 2001. As always, I was anxious to meet my new campers. I was in charge of the 10- and 11-year-old girls.

Cherish, age 11

found her under our cabin — not searching for lizards, but hiding. She did not want to go home!

A few months after camp, I managed a surprise visit to her home in California. I'll never forget the look of sheer surprise as it spread across Lizard Girl's face.

•

Jeff Wyda
was a counselor for four years.

People always ask me, "What is Camp Heartland?" And I always say, "It's heaven. It's hugs and it's smiles." These smiles last forever. They don't go away. I can't really explain it. You look around and see the magic. This is what I live for. I love Camp Heartland with all my heart. I'm a nursing student. But I've learned more from 12-year olds than I could from any textbook.

•

Lena Elliot
was a former camp director and is now
Education Programs Manager at Camp Heartland

"Hi, I'm Janet Planet," I said to a little red-headed girl, introducing my usual upbeat, friendly self. And in a scratchy, mischievous voice, she replied, "Then I'll call you 'Planet'." This one, I told myself, would be trouble.

Now, as wonderful as camp can be, it can be a difficult place for some kids. Especially kids who like to roam. This particular girl — with all the fun activities to do at camp — really liked to do only one thing: look for lizards. So keeping track of our redhead wasn't easy. We knew we could find her, somewhere, hunting for lizards. But where? That wasn't always easy to know.

But once we found her, we were in for even more surprises. I still remember the shock of finding the "pet lizard" that she kept hidden in her long, flowing, red hair.

No matter how much trouble our Lizard Girl caused us in her never-ending pursuit of little reptiles, she became one of my all time favorite people on this earth. The last day of camp I

While visiting with the Adventure Program campers and staff one afternoon on the high ropes course in Malibu, I felt a familiar change in the group's mood. It's something that happens when a participant becomes doubtful and isn't sure if they can continue along the course. Debbie, a 14-year old, sat 40 feet above us on a small platform as she talked with the facilitator about her fears — words that none of us could hear, but

Dear Mom,

I'm at camp heartland. I have some new friends. I'm having fun. I miss you. I Love you.

Bradley

sentiments all of us could feel. Half of the young people on the ground had been in that very position earlier in the day and knew that it was a tough spot.

The usual helpful prompts began — "You can do it, Debbie!"…"Go on, girl, you've got it!"…"C'mon Debbie, we're all here for you!" — as well as the soft grumblings of impatience from teenagers eager to join the rest of the campers up at the dining hall. Debbie wasn't responding, though, and it looked as if she was going to choose to end her challenge and be lowered to the ground.

Suddenly, a voice started singing, softly, from behind me. "I believe I can fly…" It was Jerome, a quiet, friendly and well-respected camper. "I believe I can touch the sky…" Everyone quieted their shouts of encouragement and looked at Jerome, who had a direct eye on Debbie, who was looking back down at him.

Others joined in: "…I think about it every night and day… Spread my wings and fly away…" And Debbie turned her eyes ahead to the ocean below the mountainside where she was perched. She said something to the facilitator that none of us could hear, gave a nod, and pushed herself off the platform, arms outstretched, eyes closed, scared — but smiling.

The group exploded with cheers. When Debbie rejoined the group, she was exhausted, but energized by her own achievement and the support and kinship of her peers.

Eric, age 13

●

George Froehle
was a college student in his first
year as a counselor.

We were in our cabin one night getting ready for bed. Our kids were loud, as usual, and we were trying to quiet them down. Kevin, who's 10, was sitting up in his bunk.

"It's time to get to bed now," I tell him.

And he says, "I know." And he lays down and looks up at me with these big eyes and asks, "Can I just go outside and look at the stars?"

"You gotta get your rest."

"I want to go see my momma," he says and starts to cry. You see, Kevin's mother and uncle both had died of AIDS.

So we went outside and stared up into the sky. And Kevin tells me how his momma is the dark star, how his uncle is the moon. And how he's the heartbeat here on earth.

"Before Momma died she said I was the heartbeat and it was up to me to keep beating…."

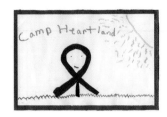

Rolling Out the Red Carpet...

...WHEN THE CAMERAS ARE OFF

Throughout the years, I have had the privilege of working with several hundred volunteers who donate their time and talents at our camp sessions and events. These everyday people help us "stretch our dollars" so we can serve even more children.

It has also been a real treat welcoming a number of celebrities to our camp sessions and fundraising events. For a child with AIDS who has been shunned by his community, a hug from a well-known star can give them great comfort. When the cameras and spotlights are off, I've had the pleasure of seeing these celebrities as they really are — compassionate and caring people.

— NEIL

David Gale: "Beavis and Butthead" to Hollywood Heart

Movie producer David Gale knows what it's like to experience illness as a child. When he was 11, he was diagnosed with Crohn's disease, an incurable disorder of the digestive system.

Looking for a way to help sick children, David contacted me in 1995. He said he wanted to get involved with Camp Heartland.

And involved he is. Summer after summer, for 11 years now, David has raised enough money to send hundreds of kids to camp in California. High above the ocean in Malibu, 100 kids each year are welcomed to a beautiful camp owned by the Wilshire Boulevard Temple.

David was the producer of movies such as "Coach Carter," "Election," "Orange County" and "Original Kings of Comedy," and executive producer of "Beavis and Butthead." He is now Executive Vice President of MTV Films.

"My business can be very caring and giving, but it can also be self-centered," he once told me. Camp Heartland is immediately satisfying. It's very tangible. It's something I can do personally to make a difference."

David spends nearly every day at camp hanging out with the kids and counselors. Each year at our celebration, MTV Night, we see him on the dance floor, rockin' with the best of them.

Because David works for MTV Films, he brings a number of movie stars to camp each year. But to the children at Camp Heartland, David Gale is always the biggest star of all.

"I Have a Dream for..."

Our summer camp in Malibu is just a half hour from L.A., and we have had visits from many Hollywood celebrities, including Brandy, Chris Tucker, Mark-Paul Gosselaar, Cuba Gooding Jr., and David Arquette. I'm grateful when celebrities drop in to meet our kids.

Yet, in August of 2001, I was especially moved to welcome to camp Martin Luther King III, the oldest son of the great civil rights leader.

I had learned much from studying about Reverend Dr. Martin Luther King, Jr. as a teenager. He had taught me that one person can make a difference and, by coming together collectively, an even greater impact can be made by many.

Dr. King's son, MLK III, visited Camp Heartland as the host of a satellite television program that profiles people whose dreams have come true. I was flattered that he wanted to create an hour-long show about my Camp Heartland dream.

I greeted him on the Malibu hillside, and when we shook hands, I was struck by how similar his eyes were to his father's. It was as if I was looking into the eyes of my hero.

Following our interview, I asked if Mr. King wanted to meet some of the campers. He was eager to meet the children, but a little thirsty.

"Do you mind if I have a can of soda," he asked.

"At camp," I said, "we avoid giving the kids soda and try to give them healthy drinks. But I'm sure I can find one can of Coke."

I found a Coke for Mr. King and we walked to the basketball courts. Suddenly, up walked Andrea, a beautiful 13-year-old African-American girl. With her exuberance and love for our camp, Andrea has always been a great ambassador for our celebrity visitors.

But this day was the exception.

Andrea looked at Mr. King, spotted his can of soda, looked at me and asked, "Why does he get a Coke?"

Blushing, I said, "Andrea, Mr. King is a very special guest today, I think it's okay to let him have a soda."

Andrea is a teenager with AIDS, but on this day she was like any other teenager with an ill-timed sense of humor. Without hesitation, she raised her arm, preacher style, looked into the eyes of the son of the greatest civil rights leader of all time and said with a fine orator's cadence, "I have a dreeeeeaam.... for a Coke."

Welcome to Camp Heartland, Mr. King!

Patricia

The Shirt Off Her Back

I met Sharon Osbourne of MTV's "The Osbournes" at a 2003 event in New York, honoring, among others, my inspiration — Nile Sandeen. Nile and Sharon's daughter, Kelly, were recognized as one of "Twenty Teens Who Are Changing the World" by Teen People magazine.

At the conclusion of the event, Sharon's publicist approached me to let me know that Sharon wanted to speak with me about Camp Heartland. I was eager for the chance to share our mission and vision with a person who was regarded as extremely kind and generous. Within the first thirty seconds of our conversation, Sharon told me she would be contributing $30,000 to Camp Heartland. I was shocked. I counted in my head the dozens of children with AIDS who would now be able to get off our waiting lists as a result of her contribution. At the end of our conversation I asked Sharon to visit our Malibu campsite. She told me she would be thrilled to meet our campers. "I'll see you this summer," she said.

Sharon was true to her word. In August of 2003, Sharon visited our California camp session. Naturally, I'm grateful to every celebrity who visits Camp Heartland. Usually, they take group photos and stay for an hour or so. But Sharon was in no rush to leave us. Despite her hectic schedule, she was happy to meet all of the 100 campers. She asked their names and gave each a warm hug. One by one, she made every camper feel special and loved.

One of the first campers Sharon met was 15-year-old Tyrone. He told Sharon that he loved her pink sweatshirt and boldly asked if he could have it. Without hesitation, Sharon took off the sweatshirt and gave it to the beaming Tyrone.

Suddenly, every kid in the room was asking Sharon for an article of her clothing. After she gave away a pricey pair of sunglasses to yet another child, I rushed to her rescue. I didn't wanted Sharon leaving Camp Heartland without any clothes!

By literally taking the shirt off her back, Sharon Osbourne demonstrated her profound love and acceptance for children with AIDS.

Host for the Day

In 1994, I asked the late camper Adam Russell to join senior director Susan Leckey and me in New York for a special event. Adam was very ill. Not only was he living with hemophilia and full-blown AIDS, but he also was struggling with cancer. He was in New York despite undergoing some powerful cancer treatments that left Adam visibly sick with pronounced sores all over his lips and mouth. I was angered by the number of people who blatantly and rudely stared at Adam during our visit to New York. I was so angry, in fact, that I confronted one individual, saying, "Take a picture. It lasts longer." I couldn't believe that people would be so insensitive to a boy who was obviously suffering greatly.

Still, Adam looked on the bright side of things. Despite his pain, he was thrilled to be in New York City, the most exciting city in the world. We attended a taping of "The Donahue Show." Adam had been a guest on the show the prior year, educating the

public about AIDS. As it turned out, Jay Leno was filming his show in New York that week, and his studio was adjacent to the Donahue studio.

We were backstage after the Donahue taping when suddenly Jay Leno walked up. He had no entourage — in fact, there was no one else in the hallway. Jay couldn't help but notice that Adam was sick. Instead of just nodding and walking by, he stopped and smiled. "Hey, you guys want a tour of the studio?" he asked. And for the next 10 minutes or so, the famous TV host became our personal tour guide, leading us around his set. On top of that, he asked Adam to sit behind his desk, while Jay occupied the guest chair.

During this pseudo interview, Adam showed us his beautiful smile again. I'm sure someone took a photograph of Adam and Jay together, but to this day I have never seen the picture. That image, though, will forever be etched in my mind.

Oprah

In 2000, I was so exceptionally pleased to be honored with the Use Your Life Award® on "The Oprah Winfrey Show." The award included a prize of $100,000, funded by Jeff Bezos of Amazon.com along with Oprah's viewers themselves who had contributed to Oprah's Angel Network. Along with the donation to Camp Heartland, I knew that appearing on Oprah's popular television program would be an ideal way to educate millions of people worldwide about children with AIDS.

True to form, Oprah's producers had created a beautiful video segment taped at the Camp Heartland Center. We had welcomed them to our Minnesota camp a month earlier and they did a fabulous job capturing the spirit of the place.

On that day, I waited backstage in Oprah's Chicago studio as the video aired, then walked into the bright stage lights to meet Oprah. As she handed me the award, I got caught up in the moment and gave Oprah a hug — only to smudge the shoulder of her black sweater with some of the makeup they make you wear when you go on television. All I could think about was that I had ruined her outfit! Would the taping stop so Oprah could change clothes? The humiliation!

She didn't even flinch. With barely a notice, she wiped away the makeup with a quick brush of her hand.

Minutes later, though, while we talked about the children, I saw her composure break slightly as she wiped tears from her face.

It was an equally emotional moment for me, and for my family — who sat in the audience that day. I was proud of how far Camp Heartland had come, but I also reflected on the loss of so many children. During my on-air conversation with Oprah, I mentioned that 15-year-old camper Daniel had recently died. Even during our happiest days, I often reflect on the children that we've lost.

Eric Waugh: the world's largest painting, 2001

At the conclusion of the show's taping, I stood backstage with my brother, Andy, and Camp Heartland camper, Jonathan. Oprah was very kind to each of us, especially young Jonathan. It was clear to me that Oprah Winfrey was the same person regardless of whether the cameras were rolling.

Through this initial television profile, along with two follow-up segments, Camp Heartland to this day still receives an outpouring of support from the viewers of "The Oprah Winfrey Show."

Eric Waugh:
A Hero in Oil Paints

Canadian painter Eric Waugh was one of the 30,000 caring supporters who contacted Camp Heartland after viewing "Angelie's Secret," a CBS documentary that featured Camp Heartland. Eric, who lives is Quebec, was so moved by the movie that he offered to donate a painting to the camp. Simply titled "Hero," hundreds of prints have since been made.

Not stopping there, Eric decided to reproduce "Hero" as a huge public mural.

Eric debuted his 41,400 square foot painting at the North Carolina Museum of Art on World AIDS Day, December 1, 2001, in Raleigh, North Carolina. Once the last of the 1,656 panels was in place, the Guinness Book of World Records made the official declaration that Eric Waugh's massive "Hero" painting was "The World's Largest Painting created by One Artist."

The painting included this touching inscription: "A week at Camp Heartland is a lifetime away from struggle for children affected by HIV and AIDS. You are invited to give these children, the real heroes, the gift of happy memories. They'll never forget you. We'll never forget them."

Eric is a true Camp Heartland champion.

Visit Eric and his artwork at *www.ericwaugh.com.*

Garth Brooks on Line Two

I was talking on the phone one day when my brother Andy rushed into my office.

"There's someone on the other line who says he's Garth Brooks," Andy said. "Do you want to talk to him?"

I laughed. Garth's foundation, Teammates for Kids, had donated $25,000 to Camp Heartland, but there was no way Garth Brooks himself would take the time to pick up the telephone and call me. It had to be a joke. After all, I had been the victim of phone pranks before by many mischievous camp counselors.

I picked up the blinking phone line to see who was on hold. "Hi, this is Neil," I said.

"Hi Neil, this is Garth Brooks," came a voice over the phone.

"Yeah, right," I said, smiling.

"Sir, this is really Garth Brooks."

I paused, feeling my jaw begin to drop. "Is this *really* Garth Brooks?"

"Neil, I have a baseball in my hand signed by Paul Molitor."

This was no joke. Baseball Hall-of-Famer Paul Molitor, a spokesman for Camp Heartland, had indeed sent Garth an autographed baseball and thank you note in appreciation of his donation.

"I-I-I'm sorry for doubting you, Mr. Brooks," I stammered. "But this probably isn't the first time someone hasn't believed it was really you on the telephone."

I thanked him for his contribution and he was very pleased to hear we had received it.

"Your music has meant a lot to me and the Camp Heartland family," I said, giving him a quick history of the organization. "The first camper we ever lost, Adam Russell, was a huge fan, and ever since I've become an admirer of you and your music as well. I use your song 'The Dance' in speeches and in eulogies."

I offered Garth the phone number of Paul Molitor, in case he wanted to give him a call. But Garth declined.

"I wouldn't know what to say to him," he humbly said, adding that he remembered Paul's amazing 39-game hitting streak in 1987. But he asked me to thank Paul for his help with Camp Heartland and for sending him the baseball.

I hung up the phone feeling a little dizzy. Despite my initial disbelief, I'd just spoken to a Camp Heartland hero, some guy named… Garth Brooks. I remain grateful and impressed that Garth had the class to thank us… for thanking him!

Jake, age 12 with Tebo

Everyday heroes: Bus Rentals and a Car-Wash Jockey

Sometimes the champions are invisible — unsung heroes who offer their compassion anonymously, yet just as sincerely.

When Camp Heartland held a family reunion on Milwaukee's lakefront, leased buses were needed to transport families north from Chicago. I was astonished when the first bus company we called offered its services for half the normal price, and rendered speechless when the second bus company offered to transport our families free of charge!

On another day a few months earlier, I dropped off the camp van for cleaning at a local car wash. When one of the employees heard that the van was owned by a HIV/AIDS organization, he offered to donate his work time and clean the van for free.

Maybe he was personally touched by AIDS, maybe he was just compassionate, I'll never know. I never got to meet the guy.

Kazumi Adachi: One Thousand Paper Cranes

On the first day of Camp Heartland's inaugural summer camp in 1993, a tiny, middle-aged Japanese woman arrived by car, unannounced and smiling brightly. Amid the chaos swirling all around, she bowed and in broken English said she was a nurse and had come to help out.

Kazumi Adachi was a beautiful person, a gentle soul who had heard of Camp Heartland in her native country.

Over the next two summers, my fondness and admiration for Kazumi grew. During a 1994 summer session of camp, she would sit on a rock near the lake making hundreds of rainbow-colored paper cranes — each one no bigger than a quarter — and connecting them together on a string. No one knew why, until the last night of camp, when she strung the cranes on the red maple tree planted in memory of camper Adam Russell. The cranes, you see, symbolized all of the children felled by AIDS.

Today, the tiny cranes hang in the home of Adam's mother, Debbie Hartway.

·

Hands-on Training

In 1994, I was at the Camp Heartland office in Minneapolis when the phone rang. It was someone from the local B'nai B'rith Youth Organization wondering if I could deliver a keynote presentation about my work with children with AIDS.

I delivered my talk and showed a few photographs of our recent summer camp session. People in the audience were very polite and seemed interested. After my speech, several gathered around and thanked me for coming. One man, Mark Margolis, and his 12-year-old son, Joe, smiled and shook my hand. They too were very polite, but as they would tell me many months later, they were also unexpectedly nervous to meet me.

Mark and Joe didn't believe I had HIV or AIDS, but were worried that they could acquire the virus from me because I worked with children who were indeed infected with the disease.

"We both went into the restroom and we washed our hands," Mark told me some time afterwards. "And we were washing our hands for an incredibly long time. Finally, my son looked at me and said, 'You know, Dad, this isn't right.'"

That moment of self-realization prompted the entire Margolis family to get involved in AIDS education. "The more we talked to people about AIDS," says Mark, "the more we saw how ignorant they were, and the more angry we got."

And soon, the Margolises became a family of advocates for Camp Heartland. They attended the camp in St. Louis, and Mark eventually was elected president of Camp Heartland's Board of Directors, helping us raise more than $1 million to obtain and renovate our camp property. Without the Margolis family, we would not have our year-round home in Willow River, Minnesota. Every visitor that enters Camp Heartland should notice that the camp is located on "Margolis Trail" in honor of this family's incredible generosity and commitment.

Today, Mark never shies away from shaking my hand — or the hand of anyone else in need.

Out of the Mouths of Babes...

To: Camp Heartland
Welcome To Our Community

We, the Tiger Scouts of Pack 3182, of Willow River, Minnesota, wish to welcome you to our community. We hope you like it here.

We had a fundraiser this fall. It was called "for the birds." We packaged and sold sunflower and mixed birdseed. It was really fun to do. We learned about work and salesmanship. We sold a lot and we are only in First Grade.

Now we are learning about the importance of helping other people. We want to give you the money we made from selling our seeds. It is $80.00. We want you to use it for fun things at your camp.

And, um, we would like to help you with your camp. We do community projects for our citizen awards. We can rake, clean up stuff, anything that would help you.

Good Luck,
The Tiger Scouts
Joey, Travis, Kasey, Beau, Zac, Rick, Cody, Mike

Dear kids at Camp Heartland

I turned 5 this year, and for my party I asked my friends to bring money instead of gifts so I could use the money to buy snacks for you. My mom found out about your camp on the internet.

I have a baby sister, and she tried to help me pack, but by accident she broke one of the snacks.

I hope you have fun at camp.
Love,
Katarena

Dear Camp Heartland,

My name is Max. I am 8 years old. I watched the television show about Angelie and her secret.

This is my allowance. I think you need it more than I do.

I feel bad for all the kids who have AIDS and are probably going to die. When I grow up I am going to be a scientist and try to create the cure for AIDS.

Yours truly,
Max

Max donated $4 of his allowance to Camp Heartland.

The Facts

HIV AND AIDS
By Darlene Baker, RN, ACRN
Camp Heartland's Healthcare & Client Services Manager

What does "HIV" and "AIDS" stand for?

HIV (Human Immunodeficiency Virus) is the name of the actual virus. AIDS (Acquired Immunodeficiency Syndrome) is the name of the condition that eventually results when HIV is either left untreated or when a person's body becomes weakened and can no longer fight off bacteria and diseases.

Are there medicines available for people living with HIV/AIDS?

Sadly, there is no cure for this disease. However, with treatment, many people with HIV or AIDS can live healthy lives. There are currently 25 drugs (24 oral medicines and one injection medicine) available to treat HIV and there is ongoing research to develop new medications and treatments.

How can a person become infected with HIV?

A person can become infected with HIV in the following ways:
- Having sexual intercourse — vaginal, anal, or perhaps oral — with an infected person.
- Sharing needles or syringes with an infected person.
- Women with HIV can pass the virus to their babies during pregnancy or birth.
- HIV can be passed from mother to infant when breast-feeding.

How do You get HIV from sexual intercourse?

HIV can be spread through unprotected anal, vaginal or oral intercourse. Contact can be from male to female, female to male or male to male. Female to female sexual transmission is possible, but rare. Unprotected sexual intercourse means sexual intercourse without correct and consistent condom use.

HIV may be found in an infected person's blood, semen, or vaginal secretions. It is thought that it can enter the body through cuts or sores — some so small you don't know they're there — on tissue in the vagina, penis, or rectum and possibly the mouth.

Since many infected people have no apparent symptoms of the condition, it's hard to be sure who is or is not infected with HIV. So, the more sex partners you have, the greater your chances of encountering a partner who is infected and becoming infected yourself.

How do you get HIV from using needles?

Sharing needles or syringes, even once, is an easy way to be infected with HIV or other bacteria/viruses. Sharing needles to inject drugs is the most dangerous form of needle sharing. Blood from an infected person can remain in or on a needle or syringe and then be transferred directly into the next person who uses it.

Sharing needles used to inject steroids or those used for tattooing or body piercing can also transmit HIV or another bacteria and viruses. If you plan to have your ears (or other body part) pierced or get a tattoo, make sure you go to a qualified technician who uses sterile equipment. Don't be shy about asking questions. Reputable technicians will explain the safety measures they follow.

Can babies be born with HIV?

A woman infected with HIV can pass the virus on to her baby during pregnancy or during birth. She can also transmit the virus when breast-feeding. If a woman is infected before or during pregnancy and she does not receive any medications, her child has about a one in four chance of being born infected. Studies have proven that if the woman takes AZT during pregnancy and/or at delivery, and the infant is treated with AZT for 6 weeks after delivery, the chances of transmission can be reduced to about 1-3%.

Any woman who is considering having a baby and who thinks she might have placed herself at risk for HIV infection — even if this occurred years ago — should seek testing and counseling before she gets pregnant. To find out where to go in your area for counseling and testing, call your local health department or the CDC National AIDS Hotline (800-342-AIDS).

Can I get HIV from a blood transfusion?

In the past, some people became infected with HIV after receiving blood transfusions. This risk has been virtually eliminated. Since 1985, all donated blood has been tested for evidence of HIV and any blood found to contain evidence of

HIV is discarded. Currently in the United States, there is almost no chance of becoming infected with HIV through a blood transfusion.

You cannot get HIV from giving blood at a blood bank or other reputable blood collection center. Needles used for blood donations are sterile, used once, then destroyed.

What are ways by which you cannot get HIV?

HIV infection doesn't just happen. You can't simply "catch" it like a cold or flu. Unlike cold or flu viruses, HIV is not spread by coughs or sneezes.

You won't get HIV through everyday contact with infected people at school, work, home, camp or anywhere else. You won't get HIV from clothes, phones, or toilet seats. HIV cannot be transmitted on items such as spoons, cups, or other objects used by someone who is infected with the virus. You won't get HIV from sweat, tears, or sneezes either.

HIV only lives inside humans (the "H" in HIV stands for Human). You can't get HIV from a mosquito bite — HIV does not live in a mosquito and it is not transmitted through a mosquito's salivary glands like other diseases such as malaria or yellow fever. You can't get it from bed bugs, lice, flies, or other insects. Other animals such as dogs and cats cannot transmit

HIV because the virus doesn't live inside their bodies.

Are medications effective in treating HIV/AIDS?

There are a lot of questions when it comes to the management of HIV/AIDS. It is important to note that, if left untreated, 95 percent of people infected with HIV will die of AIDS. The care of a person living with HIV needs to be tailored to the individual patient and needs to be based on that person's CD4 count, viral load, overall health and ability to take medications as prescribed. The idea of taking medications "for the rest of your life" is scary for some people, but it is very important that HIV medications are taken on time every day. There are currently only 25 HIV medications available. Most drug therapies involve taking two or more of these medications in different combinations to get the best health effect. If HIV medications are not taken correctly every day, it is possible that the person may become resistant to the drugs and they will no longer work (therapy failure). If the person decides in the future that he or she would like to take medications again correctly, the person may only have a limited number of medication options available.

What are the side effects of the HIV medicines?

Most medications have potential side effects. HIV medications may cause some of the following: stomach pain, nausea, vomiting, loss of appetite, taste changes, diarrhea, weakness, rashes. Some can cause dizziness, headaches, or problems sleeping.

Protease inhibitors, while very helpful to those with HIV, have other potential side effects which may be a bit more concerning. A common side effect of protease inhibitors is fat redistribution (lipodystrophy). This may include a thinning of a persons face, arms and legs and possibly fat build up in the belly, chest and upper back. Many of these drugs effect the liver (which is the body's "filter") and can cause increases in cholesterol and liver enzymes. Some protease inhibitors can cause numbness and tingling around the mouth, hands or feet. They can cause new cases of or worsening of diabetes. One protease inhibitor, Crixivan, can cause kidney stones (so it is important that someone who is taking this medicine drinks lots of water).

Can you be friends with someone who has HIV/AIDS?

I have had the pleasure of working as a nurse on the Camp Heartland medical team for over six years. During that time, I have held children when they felt sick, tended to their cuts and scrapes, administered IV and injection medications and given prescribed medicines to children, most of whom have HIV in their bodies. I have held their hands, played games, gone for walks and shared meals with children at camp. I am HIV negative and have never felt I was at risk of getting HIV from anyone I've cared for, because I know that HIV cannot be transmitted casually and, as a healthcare worker, I use common sense and Standard Precautions (hand washing and gloves for example). By learning the facts about HIV and AIDS, you can become aware of how a person can and can't get HIV.

(Sources: Centers for Disease Control and Prevention (CDC). National Center for HIV, STD, and TB Prevention, Divisions of HIV/AIDS Prevention, Updated November 2, 1998.)

Where can I learn more about HIV/AIDS?

There are many resources available for those interested in gaining more knowledge about the disease. Please call the CDC National AIDS Hotline at 800-342-AIDS (2437) or visit the following Web sites:

Camp Heartland *www.campheartland.org*
The Body *www.thebody.com*
Centers for Disease Control *www.cdc.gov*
National Association of People with AIDS *www.napwa.org*
National Minority AIDS Council *www.nmac.org*
Women, Children, and HIV *www.womenchildrenhiv.org*
National Pediatric and Family HIV Resource Center
www.pedhivaids.org
Project Inform *www.projinf.org*

Jake, age 12, takes his medications

Camp Heartland

HOW YOU CAN MAKE A DIFFERENCE

What is the mission of Camp Heartland?

Camp Heartland is a national 501(c)3 non-profit organization that enhances the lives of children infected with and affected by HIV/AIDS through year-round support, advocacy, recreational programs and community AIDS awareness efforts.

What programs and services does Camp Heartland offer?

CAMP HEARTLAND SUMMER CAMPS and REUNION PROGRAMS — Through our week-long summer camping programs and year-round "mini-session" reunions, we help the children make friends, have fun and develop new skills and self confidence. The development of The Camp Heartland Center allows us to welcome thousands of children throughout the year.

LIFE ENHANCEMENT PROGRAMS — Our Life Enhancement programs are designed to sustain and build upon the experiences gained at summer camp. Through various educational, recreational and social opportunities — including day trips, special mailings and regular contact with camp staff — campers are able to remain connected to Camp Heartland throughout the year and maintain the unique support network they developed during the summer.

CAMP HEARTLAND SHARES — Through our Camp Heartland Shares program, our medical, psychosocial and camping professionals provide comprehensive information, printed materials, and technical support to agencies and individuals interested in initiating their own HIV camping programs. Several new camps have been initiated through this unique support program.

HEARTLAND PARTNERS — Camp Heartland partners with other organizations that assist underserved populations to provide a camping program for their own clients. Our highly skilled and well-trained staff is utilized to develop and implement a program specifically designed for each Heartland Partner agency.

JOURNEY OF HOPE AIDS AWARENESS PROGRAMS — Since 1993, Camp Heartland has been a leader in HIV/AIDS awareness efforts. The Journey of Hope AIDS Awareness Program is a unique presentation that features speeches, skits, and poetry by the children and young adults of Camp Heartland. Many of our Journey of Hope speakers are profiled in this book. During their presentations, the children share their own personal stories and messages about HIV/AIDS. The program is often described as "powerful and inspiring."

The Journey of Hope speakers want you to know:

- **Acquired Immune Deficiency Syndrome (AIDS) is preventable.** Human Immunodeficiency Virus (HIV), the virus that causes AIDS, is only transmitted through infected blood, semen, vaginal secretions and breast milk. Avoid sharing HIV contaminated needles, having unprotected sexual contact, and direct (blood to blood) contact with HIV infected blood to reduce your risk of exposure to HIV.
- **HIV is not transmitted casually.** It's safe to be a friend to someone who is HIV positive or has AIDS. You can hold hands, hug, play sports, drink from the same water fountain, swim in the same pool and many more everyday activities that friends share.

- **You should be empathetic.** Until there is a cure for HIV/AIDS, the one thing we can all do to help those who live with this disease is to be a friend. Listen, share, respect and show compassion to those infected or affected by the virus.
- **All people with HIV and AIDS deserve compassion.** At Camp Heartland, we don't believe AIDS is a punishment or that anyone deserves to have AIDS. Regardless of how HIV is contracted all people deserve to live with dignity and respect.
- **You should get tested.** If you have ever had unprotected sex or have shared needles, it is important to get tested. Teens and young adults account for more than half of the new

How much does Camp Heartland charge each family for our programs?

As the majority of our campers live in poverty, all of our programs and services are provided free of charge. Camp Heartland must raise $3,000 per child for a year's worth of programs and services.

How does Camp Heartland raise money?

Camp Heartland relies on the generosity of thousands of donors to make our programs and services possible. From children donating their allowances to philanthropists contributing six figure gifts, Camp Heartland exists through the generosity of thousands of donors annually.

What companies and foundations support Camp Heartland?

Some of our most generous contributors include Argent Mortgage Company, Wisconsin Hospitality Group — Pizza Hut, Cities 97 radio station in Minneapolis, Miller Brewing Company, Fallon advertising agency, Northwestern Mutual Foundation, Direct Supply, the Hillis Family, and Northwest Airlines and Hollywood Heart.

HIV/AIDS cases in the United States and many may be unaware of their HIV status. For information on anonymous and confidential testing sites in your community, call the National HIV Hotline at 800-342-AIDS or visit *www.hivtest.org.*

How do I bring a Camp Heartland Journey of Hope AIDS Awareness Program to my community?

If you are interested in bringing the Journey of Hope AIDS Awareness Program to your community please contact: 800-724-4673.

Who do I contact to sign my child up for Camp Heartland?

Your child may be able to attend Camp Heartland if he/she is living with HIV/AIDS, has an immediate family member with the disease or has lost a loved one to AIDS. Please contact the Camper Registration Department at 888-216-2028

How do I make a contribution to Camp Heartland?

If you are moved and inspired by our children, we welcome you to become a supporter of our non-profit organization. All contributions to Camp Heartland are tax-deductible within the full extent of the law. You can mail your check or money order to:

Camp Heartland, "A Journey of Hope"
1845 N. Farwell Avenue, Suite 310 • Milwaukee, WI 53202

You can donate online at: *www.campheartland.org*
You can donate by telephone at: 800-724-4673

Does Camp Heartland accept in-kind support?

We rely on extensive in-kind support to keep our administrative costs low. Thousands of items are donated each year — from gift cards to disposable cameras. Our donors range from young children who contribute snacks to flower shops like Arts and Flowers in Minnesota who created a red ribbon bouquet of hundreds of roses for the funeral of one of our participants. A "wish list" of desired items can be found at *www.campheartland.org*

How can young people support Camp Heartland?

Camp Heartland receives the support of thousands of students nationwide. Through our "Students for Camp Heartland" program, dozens of student groups raise awareness of HIV/AIDS and funding for Camp Heartland. The largest student contributions come from Greek Week at the University of Michigan and Humorology at the University of Wisconsin. If you are interested in being a part of Students for Camp Heartland please contact the Student Coordinator at 888-216-2028.

How do I become a volunteer for Camp Heartland?

If you would like a volunteer application, please contact 800-724-4673 or *www.campheartland.org*

Is the Camp Heartland Center available for rental?

Yes. Dozens of groups ranging from youth groups to corporations rent our camp for retreats, family reunions, challenge course outings and camp sessions. To rent The Camp Heartland Center please call 888-545-6658.

Where can I buy additional copies of this book?

Please contact 800-724-4673 to order additional copies of *A Journey of Hope.*

Where will the profits be contributed from this book?

Because *A Journey of Hope* was underwritten by a foundation, all proceeds directly benefit Camp Heartland's programs, services and, ultimately, our children.

In the early days of Camp Heartland, we held candlelight vigils at each week-long camp as a way to give voice to our campers. Most of our kids are forced to live very private lives, and just the experience of coming to Camp Heartland is liberating. These evening vigils at the end of the week were both celebratory and sad, and served as the perfect time to free up their thoughts and feelings.

In our second summer, we spent a week at a beautiful camp in the woods near Blairstown, New Jersey. Cabins of white clapboard faced a small lake. Campers caught salamanders and tadpoles in their bare hands in the weeds.

On the last night of camp, 100 campers congregated on a hillside by the lake for our final candlelight vigil. Small candles on paper plates were set afloat on the still lake. Dozens more spelled out the words "Camp Heartland" on the grassy shore. Counselors and parents silently encircled the children. And, as the sky darkened, everyone was given a small candle to tend to.

"This is the time to be happy," I told the kids as they stared into their flames. "This is the time for us to make a wish, because all of us, all of us have a bright future. Everybody's doing well, and there's hope in the world."

One by one, around the circle, the campers spoke up.

"I miss my whole family," began one little girl, fighting back tears. "My mom died. My mom and dad and my brother died, a long time ago. But my new mom said I look exactly like my real mom."

Said another little girl: "I just love every one of you guys, because I know what you're going through."

"I hope you all had fun at Camp Heartland," added a boy. "I know I did. And I hope you'll be here next year. I'll be here as long as possible."

And lifting our candles to the sky, we made our wishes....

How the Candle Became our Symbol

As the vigil ended, campers embraced counselors, brothers hugged sisters, and fireworks suddenly brightened the sky above. Finally, after an outpouring of raw emotion, the counselors led the children to their cabins for a snack before bedtime. The parents, meanwhile, remained at the lakeside, silently milling around, still holding onto their candles. I could hear some of them sobbing. I could tell they were upset by the some of the stories that were told during the vigil.

One by one, they began sharing their own stories, sad stories of guilt and grief and fear of the future, of how they were infected with HIV, of how their children were infected. This was a first-time experience for many of them, and emotions flowed. It was empowering, vital, necessary, sorrowful — all of these things at once.

By now, it was quite late. The size of the group had dwindled, and the wind had picked up. We had become a huddled mass down on the bottom of the hillside. One mother took her turn, stepping up and looking deeply into the candle that she held. Her 14-year-old son's immune system was perilously crippled, and we all worried that he would become terribly ill.

The mother stared at the flame, tears welling her eyes. Wax dripped between her fingers. "This candle's getting shorter and shorter and shorter," she said finally, and nothing more. Everyone knew what she meant.

Suddenly, thank God, out of the shadows emerged a little boy who had strayed from his cabin and wandered down to the lakeside. He had been listening to the parents for awhile. I had seen him out of the corner of my eye. He was a boy with hemophilia and AIDS, 10-years old, but very small for his age. He had a horrible hemophilia bleed that he didn't tell us about and was limping.

He approached the front of the group, this little boy, and in a soft but deliberate voice, he spoke: "The candle is getting shorter. But it's still lit. It still burns, it still lights the dark. The flame is alive. There's still hope."

— NEIL